GRATEFUL AND GIVING

*How Msgr. Thomas McGread's Stewardship
Message Has Impacted Catholic Parishes
Throughout the Country*

Deacon Donald R. McArdle

Grateful and Giving

Copyright © 2011 by Deacon Donald R. McArdle

ISBN 978-0-615-47175-4

*For Monsignor Thomas McGread,
a faithful follower of Jesus Christ*

*He has had a tremendous impact on the Church
in the United States and beyond. May his impact
continue to be felt throughout the world as we
embrace Stewardship as a way of life.*

ACKNOWLEDGMENTS

There are many people who contributed to the development of this book. I have listed below the key contributors without whom this book would not have been possible.

First, I would like to extend my sincerest gratitude to Msgr. Thomas McGread. I thank him for his example and for his willingness to help with this project. His willingness to share with me was invaluable as I put this book together. And I can't ignore thanking him for being a friend and a mentor to me in the development of this book and many other ways.

I want to thank two of my daughters, Tricia McArdle Sherman and Shauna McArdle Occhipinti, who were the key instruments in putting the bulk of this book together. They worked tirelessly on draft after draft of this book and without their skill and hard work this book would have never been done.

I want to thank Stan Byrdy who did a lot of the initial work on gathering and assembling material to get the initial form and substance of this book together.

I want to thank all of the Catholic Stewardship Consultant staff members who participated in one way or another on this book – particularly, my son, Eric McArdle, Fletcher Bingham, and Rob Mueller. Their willingness to review and edit the book was a great help.

I cannot forget the many folks in the Diocese of Wichita and particularly at St. Francis of Assisi whose experience and faithfulness to God provided the substance of this book. In particular, I'd like to thank those who shared the stories of their Stewardship journeys with me and helped me gather the necessary information for this book. To Bishop Eugene Gerber, Dan Loughman, Paul and Bettie Eck, Fr. John Lanzrath, and Sr. Stephanie Heskamp, ASC - thank you.

I also want to thank some of my fellow clergymen who work to implement the Stewardship way of life in their parishes and willingly shared their stories. I am confident that their experiences will impact many people through this book. Thank you Msgr. Jim Costigan, Msgr. Chester Borski, Fr. Allan McDonald and Fr. David Zimmer.

Thanks to Ricardo Silva, the talented graphic designer who skillfully created the beautiful cover design.

And last, but most certainly not least, I thank my wife, Pat. Her love and encouragement throughout the writing of this book increased my determination to complete it. I couldn't have done it without her.

A MEDITATION

By: Eugene J. Gerber, Bishop Emeritus of Wichita

Prime among the many gifts that come with being created in God's image and likeness is the capacity 'to give' and 'to receive'

Stewardship helps us to discover our vocation and live it, identify our personal dignity, and respect it, recognize God's prompting and embrace it. Moreover, it "helps to rouse one another to love and good works" (Heb. 10:24). Everyone, regardless of circumstances, has something to give to others and is in need of receiving from others for the glory of God and the salvation of the human family.

The word "stewardship" may be new to some, but the living of it is as old as the creation of Adam and Eve. It was not, could not be, lost by original sin. How could God not always desire the beauty of giving what we have received and receiving of what others have been given? Stewardship, then, is not a mere human invention, nor a mere human message, nor, yet, a mere human witness.

Jesus is always present drawing us more nearly, more dearly, more clearly into the mutual reciprocal and interdependent relationships which the Father, the Son, and the Holy Spirit enjoy without beginning or end.

This eternal joy "to the full" is the destiny of every person without exception. While on our pilgrim way, stewardship, embraced as a way of life, increases our awareness of how God is drawing us to Himself and how He is making life-giving connections with others. The greater the awareness, the greater the marvel; the greater the marvel, the greater the gratitude.

Many times in His preaching Jesus proclaimed and witnessed to the imperative of being a worthy steward of our time, talent, and gifts, not as slaves, but as friends (Jn. 15). At the Last Supper, Jesus gave the apostles, and all of us, a powerful example when He lovingly stooped to wash their feet. Then He said: "Do you understand what I have done for you? ... If I, Lord and Master, have washed your feet, you should wash each other's feet" (Jn. 13:13-14). We do well to keep our eyes fixed on Him and to receive His look of love, even to fervently pray for it.

The "timing" for today's Stewardship came in the wake of the Second Vatican Council's universal call to holiness. It is a call that is necessary in order to build a civilization of love in a secularized society guided by unhealthy individualism.

The Stewardship way of life model that Msgr. Thomas McGread developed is not the only one, but it is clearly the most enduring and proven one. It is one that many parishes across the Church in the United States have found practical, adaptable and viable, keeping the essential elements intact, of course. It is a proven model on which we in the Diocese of Wichita were able to draw when our 1985 Diocesan Pastoral Plan called for the launching of United Catholic Stewardship as a priority for our parishes, schools, and institutions.

You will discover practical, personal, and essential elements of the universal call to holiness in this work by Deacon Don McArdle paying tribute to Msgr. McGread. From my perspective, Msgr. McGread is an instrument of the Lord in developing a model of living biblical Stewardship in our era.

This book is a tribute, not only to Msgr. McGread, but also to the many lay people who worked so closely with him, giving generously of their time, talent, and daily experience of lived Stewardship. With the passage of time, this number of nameless lay people working with other pastors and bishops has ballooned to countless persons living life closer to the Lord and the Church with grateful hearts.

I pray that God the Father will grace the words of this work as you reflect on its content and that the Holy Spirit will increase your awareness of the Lord's loving presence with you as you "place your gifts at the service of others" (1Pt. 4:10) and in return experience the satisfaction of receiving more than you give.

CONTENTS

INTRODUCTION

What does it mean to be a "Disciple of Jesus Christ"? When many of us hear the word "disciple," our minds turn to images we have seen of the early Church disciples, beautiful and sometimes very ornate icons, pictures, statues and stained glass windows depicting those first disciples. It is hard for us to relate to them. We read the story of Pentecost in Acts of the Apostles, and we are left in awe of the courage and boldness of those early disciples who were called and sent by God to proclaim the "Good News." We go on to read in Acts and elsewhere in the New Testament how these early disciples went forward from Pentecost with courage and boldness to continue the ministry of Jesus through what they said and did, how they lived and died.

Yet we all know that before Pentecost these same disciples were not a picture of courage and boldness. The reason they were hiding in the Upper Room on that first Pentecost was because they were afraid of what the authorities would do to them if they were caught and identified with Jesus. And they had good reason to fear. What's more, as they walked with Jesus before His passion, they did not display the same courage, boldness and understanding that they did after Pentecost. So, it's not as though the early disciples were superhumans to whom we have nothing in common. Quite the opposite, in fact. They gained their courage and boldness from the Lord. On Pentecost, Jesus sent the Holy Spirit upon them, filling them with a sense of mission. On Pentecost they became changed people, not because they read a book or got a degree in theology, but because they were filled with the Holy Spirit; the third person of the Blessed Trinity. As they went forth from Pentecost and allowed the Spirit of God to work through them, they not only continued the ministry of Jesus, but they became more and more an extension of Jesus.

Being a disciple of Jesus Christ is a fundamental part of our individual identity. It may be formed, in part, by the family or groups we belong to, by our education or our profession, or by our hobbies. However, as baptized and confirmed Catholics, the most fundamental part of our identity should be living as "Disciples of Jesus Christ" who love one another. In fact, in the Gospel according to Luke, Jesus is quoted using some very strong language, making the point that to be His disciple comes before everything, and by that He means everything in our lives. "If anyone comes to me without hating father and mother, wife and children, brothers and sisters, and even his own life, he cannot be my disciple" (Lk. 14:26). This means, if I am a disciple of Jesus, how I think, what I believe and how I act should be guided by the Gospel and not by the secular culture.

The practice of Stewardship as a way of life, as described in this book, changes lives by helping each of us grow in our understanding of discipleship and in our living as a disciple of Jesus. Stewardship, in reality, is all about living out the Sacraments of Baptism, Confirmation, and Eucharist. Stewardship is about living as Disciples of Jesus, just like those early disciples did – with courage and boldness. Christ's work of building the Church continues today, and we are the ones He has called and equipped to go forth and do His work.

I wrote this book to explain what I understand to be the roots of Stewardship as currently being practiced in the Catholic Church in the United States and to help pastors and lay leaders to understand what living Stewardship can do for their parishioners, their parishes, their dioceses, the wider Church and society in general.

I first recognized the far-reaching impact that Stewardship can have on one's faith life, on the lives of parishes and dioceses and even the Church at-large during my first visit to the Catholic Diocese of Wichita, Kansas. Msgr. Thomas McGread, a renown stewardship pioneer, showed me the many facilities and introduced me to some of the people through which the diocese carries out Stewardship on a daily basis.

After just a short visit, it was obvious that the Diocese of Wichita was not like any other diocese that I have known. In addition to having a place for the diocesan offices in downtown Wichita, the diocese also owns a 240-acre campus where they provide a 186-bed nursing home, a 60-bed assisted-living center, a 40-bed memory care center for those with dementia, and a retreat center that can host 116 overnight guests at any one time. The large diocesan campus is a sight to behold. The buildings are beautifully constructed. The landscaped grounds include a serene pond, life-sized Stations of the Cross, shrines, and much more.

Except for the Memory Care Center, which was constructed with industrial revenue bonds, every bit of the diocesan campus was built with the generous gifts of the people of the Diocese of Wichita – a Stewardship people! As a result of diocesan-wide Stewardship (which they call United Catholic Stewardship) over the years, they have offered their time, talent and treasure to ensure that all of this was built and staffed in an effort to love and care for their brothers and sisters in Christ and others in need.

Msgr. McGread also showed me the Lord's Diner, a soup kitchen run by the diocese; the Guadalupe Clinic, a medical clinic for the underprivileged, which is staffed almost entirely by volunteers; and he showed me around the campus of the Catholic Life Center.

I was blown away at all I saw.

Yet it is not just the generous amounts of money that the diocese is regularly gifted or even the many different opportunities that such money affords them that makes the Diocese of Wichita stand out. In fact, as you tour the grounds of what is affectionately named, "The Catholic Life Center" what stands out much brighter than the many buildings and the grounds are the people and the love they have for Christ, which is experienced through the level of hospitality and general friendliness. Their lives are a witness to the Gospel, and their constant smiles and joyful "hellos" speak volumes. They live to serve Christ and to serve others as His disciples, and they love doing so. And that – above all else – is what makes the Diocese of Wichita a Stewardship diocese.

During my first visit, Msgr. McGread told me story after story about how, through the diocese's 1985 Stewardship initiative called United Catholic Steward-ship, which continues today, the diocese has been able to run the different facilities, thanks to the generosity of the people. He assured me that Stewardship has not only enabled the diocese to build and staff the many care centers, but that living Stewardship, real biblical Stew-ardship, has changed the hearts and minds of the people throughout the diocese. In fact, it is precisely because of this change of heart and the people's commitment to live Stewardship as a way of life, serving Christ as His disci-ples today, that the diocese has been able to do so much.

In all of my travels from diocese to diocese over the years, I have never seen anything like it. But it is im-portant to start at the beginning.

My amazement heightened when Msgr. McGread brought me to St. Francis of Assisi Church, the beginning of it all. It was as pastor of that average-sized parish, which at the time of Msgr. McGread's pastorate included about 1,500 parishioners, that Msgr. McGread first saw the Stewardship way of life flourish for the people of Wichita. It was there, within the life of that "normal" parish family, that the idea of living discipleship through the practice of Stewardship was first understood, embraced, and modeled in this now renowned Stewardship diocese.

As I looked around, I noticed the small stone Stations of the Cross that hung humbly on the wall. I noticed the simply constructed pews and the carpeted floor. The more I noticed, the more I realized, this church is just like any other!

Yet, by all accounts, St. Francis is not just like any other parish. They are a normal middle-class parish, yes, but, the more I discovered about the life of St. Francis of Assisi parish, the more I realized how extraordinary it is.

Eighty-five percent of the registered parishioners are active, meaning that they attend Mass every Sunday, they participate in one or more parish ministries, and they give financially to the parish. Meanwhile, the average percentage of active parishioners in Catholic parishes around the country is about 30%. What's more, with 2,500 registered households at the time of my visit, St. Francis was seeing a weekly offertory of about $90,000.

The more I learned, the more I was amazed.

What is it that accounts for the many good things happening at St. Francis and, really, all throughout the Diocese of Wichita? They are living the Stewardship way of life. They are ordinary Catholics living ordinary lives. Yet they recognize their "ordinary lives" as extraordinary gifts from an ever-gracious God, so they use their lives – everything they have (their time, their talent, and their treasure) – to serve Him. And so it is that the Steward-ship way of life has changed the spirituality of the diocese.

I left Wichita with a reinforced conviction. I already believed that living our call to discipleship through the Stewardship way of life was necessary for all Catholics, but during that brief visit to Wichita, the Holy Spirit energized me. I wanted to be a part of spreading the message of Stewardship. I wanted to show Catholics around the nation, and even the world, that Stewardship will change their dioceses and their parishes, but more specifically that Stewardship will change the hearts of the people, bringing them to a deeper appreciation of who they are as disciples and stewards of all God's gifts.

For the past 11 years now, we, at Catholic Steward-ship Consultants, have been working with Msgr. McGread in an attempt to spread the Stewardship message. We have devoted our work to helping pastors and parish leaders implement the Stewardship way of life in their parishes, and we have seen it bear fruit in many lives. I have seen conversion take place in the lives of many people (including pastors). And as the people live their lives more committed as disciples of Christ today, it has renewed the lives of their parishes.

There is no doubt that the practice of Biblical Stewardship changes people's hearts. I hope that this book will help you understand just how that change takes place. Looking to Msgr. McGread, a modern day pioneer of Stewardship as a way of life, as an example, I pray that many pastors and lay leaders will come to recognize the importance of making Stewardship the foundational principle of all parish life and ministry.

This book will also provide pastors and lay leaders with a description of tools and processes used to initiate and sustain a vibrant parish Stewardship initiative.

Christ calls each one of us to Himself as His disciples. May we embrace that call with courage and use all that we have been given – our time, our talents, our treasure, our very lives as a whole – selflessly, in the service of Christ whom we follow. We are but present-day disciples. May we all live as such!

"Once one chooses to become a disciple of Jesus Christ, Stewardship is not an option."

-USCCB, Stewardship a Disciple's Response

PART I

WHAT IS STEWARDSHIP?

CHAPTER 1

STEWARDSHIP UNCOVERED

"A Stewardship way of life is a thanksgiving way of life, living life as God intended it to be lived," Msgr. Thomas McGread joyfully proclaims in August 2004 to a crowd of about 150 Catholic priests and lay parish leaders who are perched on the edge of their seats, eager to absorb his message. The men and women are gathered in a beautifully decorated conference room, surrounded by life-like icons depicting the 33 Doctors of the Church. You can see the love in St. Therese's eyes as she grips the cross of her savior tightly. The profound faith of St. Leo the Great is quite clear as, robed in beautiful gold vestments, he lifts the Eucharist for all to see. Even the silver streaks in St. Cyril's beard are detectable. Yet these saints are not the focal point. Conference participants are awestruck by the five-foot-nine priest who preaches a life-changing message. The power and conviction with which he preaches makes even the most disinterested conference participant fix his gaze and grasp his pen, frantically trying to jot down Msgr. McGread's every word. "Embrace Stewardship as a way of life," Msgr. McGread tells the crowd, "and you will never be the same!"

Msgr. McGread believes this with all of his heart. He has witnessed the Stewardship way of life change the hearts and minds of his parishioners, and he knows, in the depths of his heart, that if Stewardship is embraced by all, the Church will more powerfully live Christian discipleship today.

Msgr. McGread's personal journey with Stewardship began when he was a young child. Though he did not identify it as a "Stewardship journey," the seeds of faith that Msgr. McGread's parents planted in him from his earliest years had a big impact on the life he would lead and the change he would make in the life of the Church.

"Dad and Mom both taught me what it means to be a disciple of Jesus," Msgr. McGread admits with great gratitude. "I can remember Dad making it a point to take care of many people. Especially if someone died or someone was ill, he would go to the grocery store, and bring people food, and he would make sure to be available to them whenever he saw a need. Serving others was a part of my upbringing. Mom and Dad were teaching me early on that the life of a Christian is a life of service – to God and one another."

Msgr. McGread also recalls nightly prayers with his parents and his five siblings.

"The Rosary was a requirement in our house," he says. "We prayed together every day, and we understood very young that prayer was a vital part of our Catholic life."

It was with this firm foundation that Msgr. McGread was open to the Lord's call for him to be a priest. In fact, his uncle was a priest, so he knew that, while it was a demanding way of life, it was a beautiful response to Christ's call in his life, and he was eager to respond.

He attended seminary in Dublin, Ireland and was subsequently ordained for the Diocese of Wichita.

"Everyone in my seminary was going to serve some-where else in the world, and I had been asked to serve in the United States in the Diocese of Wichita," Msgr. McGread remembers. And so the little Irish priest came to America where his life and many of our lives were changed forever – thanks to the work of the Holy Spirit in the life of this self-giving servant.

In 1959, Msgr. McGread's Stewardship journey took a new path. He came across the manuscript for a book by two priests, Fr. Joseph Jennings and Fr. David Sullivan, from the Diocese of Mobile, Alabama and he was struck with an "a ha" moment. "They were trying to come up with a Catholic theology for the Protestant idea of tithing," recalls Msgr. McGread. The concept piqued his interest, so Msgr. McGread proceeded through the draft, not knowing then that it would drastically change his life and ministry.

How he even received a draft of their book, *Tithing,* remains a mystery. "Maybe the Holy Spirit had something to do with it," he remarks. "It was actually addressed to a classmate of one of the priests in Mobile whose name was McGready. I happened to get it after several corrections, but I didn't know where it came from. There was really nothing in the package but this little book about tithing, so I read it."

That day stands as a monumental turning point not only for Msgr. McGread, but for the Church at large. What Msgr. McGread read struck a chord with him. It pushed him to look at tithing differently, and it was this new outlook, this deeper understanding that would eventually impact the community of St. Francis of Assisi, the Diocese of Wichita, and beyond.

"One of the things I noticed in their writings," Msgr. McGread says, "was that there was a tremendous emphasis on the fact that people are looking for standards in life – the type of home they live in, the type of education their children receive, and the various ways that they live."

And that got Msgr. McGread thinking.

"If we're looking for standards in life," he explains, "we also must be looking for standards in our relationship with God." So, he started talking to his parishioners about setting standards for their relationship with the Lord. At the outset, because of the reading he had done, most of these talks were focused mainly on tithing.

Until ...

"I noticed that whenever you mentioned tithing in church you lost over 50% of the audience right away," Msgr. McGread recalls.

And then, a "eureka" moment!

Tithing was a spiritual standard that was practiced most successfully in Protestant churches, but Msgr. McGread wanted to encourage his parishioners to find standards that went beyond their financial gifts. It was then that he began working to develop the concepts of time and talent as the foundation for the treasure portion of the equation in living a life of Stewardship.

"I realized there must be more to this idea of building a relationship with God," he remembers. "So that's when I came up with the idea that all of us have a certain amount of time in this world, and all of us have a certain amount of talents." It was this realization that led Msgr. McGread to explore the ways in which we as Christians ought to cultivate our relationship with God and live discipleship today.

How, you may wonder, does the mere fact that we all have time and talents – a reality that no one would or could deny – have an immediate bearing on the way in which a Christian is to live? It all hinges on recognizing that everything we have are all gifts from God – our time and our talents, even our very lives. We ought to consider, everyday, how we use all that we have been given.

The average person spends 25,000 days on Earth. When we meet the Lord on the last day of our life here, we must account for how we spent those days. Did we recognize the gifts God had given us and use them for His glory, to draw others to Him and build the kingdom here on Earth? Or did we take what He gave us for granted and use it for personal gain, simply waste it, or bury it?

That is where the Stewardship way of life – the life of a Christian disciple – begins.

While Msgr. McGread developed certain concepts behind living the Stewardship way of life today and implementing that way of life in modern Catholic parishes, Stewardship wasn't his idea. It was God's idea! From the very beginning, even before the fall of Adam and Eve, God has called man to care for and cultivate the gifts he has been given.

> *"Be fertile and multiply; fill the earth and subdue it. Have dominion over the fish of the sea, the birds of the air, and all the living things that move on the earth. ... See, I give you every seed-bearing plant all over the earth and every tree that has seed-bearing fruit on it to be your food"*
>
> *(Gen. 1:28-29).*

And we all know the parable of the talent:

> *"It will be as when a man who was going on a journey called in his servants and entrusted his possessions to them. To one he gave five talents; to another, two; to a third, one--to each according to his ability. Then he went away. Immediately the one who received five talents went and traded with them, and made another five. Likewise, the one who received two made another two. But the man*

who received one went off and dug a hole in the ground and buried his master's money. After a long time the master of those servants came back and settled accounts with them. The one who had received five talents came forward bringing the additional five. He said, 'Master, you gave me five talents. See, I have made five more.' His master said to him, 'Well done, my good and faithful servant. Since you were faithful in small matters, I will give you great responsibilities. Come, share your master's joy.' (Then) the one who had received two talents also came forward and said, 'Master, you gave me two talents. See, I have made two more.' His master said to him, 'Well done, my good and faithful servant. Since you were faithful in small matters, I will give you great responsibilities. Come, share your master's joy.' Then the one who had received the one talent came forward and said, 'Master, I knew you were a demanding person, harvesting where you did not plant and gathering where you did not scatter; so out of fear I went off and buried your talent in the ground. Here it is back.' His master said to him in reply, 'You wicked, lazy servant! So you knew that I harvest where I did not plant and gather where I did not scatter? Should you not then have put my money in the bank so that I could have got it back with interest on my return? Now then! Take the talent from him and give it to the one with ten. For to everyone who has, more will be given and he will grow rich; but from the one who has not, even what he has will be taken away."

(Mt. 25:14-30)

The concept of true Christian Stewardship is, in fact, biblically-rooted. Msgr. McGread would never deny that. In fact, when Msgr. McGread gives a talk on the Stewardship way of life, he is never seen without his Bible. "The textbook for Christian Stewardship is the holy Bible," Msgr. McGread says, clutching his New American Bible, whose jacket is worn from the many years of use.

So it's not as if Msgr. McGread discovered something new when he opened that book, *Tithing*, over 50 years ago. Rather, he simply rediscovered the call to discipleship, the call that God has placed on the hearts of human beings since the beginning of time. But what Msgr. McGread did discover is that when we live the call to discipleship through Stewardship, when we recognize everything we have as gifts from God and we use all of it for His glory, God will work in us to change our hearts and the hearts of those around us. Stewardship will draw us into a deeper relationship with Him.

"Since the beginning of time, human beings have been trying to come up with ideas of things that will bring them happiness," Msgr. McGread explains. "For some it was power, for some it was drugs, for some it was alcohol, for some it was sex. Yet none of those things have ever really satisfied people. They don't last for any length of time. That is simply because God made all of us in the same way. He made us to be united with Him, and unless we live for Him, we will be unhappy. The only time we are going to be truly happy in this life is when we have a personal relationship with God, and we are living our lives in His service. And that is what Stewardship is all about."

Convinced that Stewardship was the proper way of life for every Christian, Msgr. McGread wasted no time implementing it in his parishes.

During the early years of his priesthood, he was assigned to a patchwork of parishes scattered throughout the Diocese of Wichita. Bishop Mark Carroll first assigned him as associate pastor at St. Patrick's in Parsons, Kansas. Then, the bishop moved him to what Msgr. McGread recalls as "a plot of land." There was no building there at the time, and Msgr. McGread's assignment required him to help the pastor start from scratch and establish a parish family. After three years, St. Anne's parish was built on that "plot of land", and the bishop moved Msgr. McGread again. This time, he was assigned to "yet another plot of land," he remembers. "So I started there again." Msgr. McGread successfully assisted the pastor in the building of St. Jude's parish before the bishop moved him again. "This time he moved me to a little place outside of Wichita to build a new church down in Erie,

Kansas and serve as its pastor," Msgr. McGread says. Two years later, after St. Ambrose was established, the bishop assigned Msgr. McGread to the Church of the Resurrection parish, which, at the time, was yet another "plot of land".

"I spent three years at Resurrection where I helped build a church and a school from the ground up," he remembers.

Time and again, as the bishops moved him from place to place, Msgr. McGread rose to the challenges that each assignment presented. As he moved around the diocese and established parish after parish, Msgr. McGread did his best to sow the seeds of Stewardship in the hearts of his people. It wasn't easy though. In addition to overseeing the building of these parishes, Msgr. McGread faced the challenge of implementing the Stewardship way of life amidst such small and newly established communities, that he did not see much impact. Yet, he did not let that deter him. Msgr. McGread knew that, as a pastor, his mission was to bring people closer to Christ, to call them on as disciples of Jesus. In parish after parish, year after year, he continued to do just that.

In 1968, when Bishop David Maloney transferred him to St. Francis of Assisi in Wichita, Kansas, life was not about to get any easier. In fact, the move to St. Francis would prove to be the most challenging of Msgr. McGread's young priesthood. There, faced with particularly dire circumstances, Msgr. McGread would be asked to build the Church in an even greater way than his prior assignments had required. Much akin to the patron saint of the parish, Msgr. McGread would need to revive the faith of his people. He would need to "rebuild the Church" much like St. Francis was asked to do many years ago.

Bishop Maloney must have been lead by the Holy Spirit in his decision, because there is no doubt that Msgr. McGread was up for the challenge. In fact, he not only served to build the faith of his people, making the parish a strong and vibrant parish family, he sowed seeds of faith that have become the proverbial tree from the mustard seed.

CHAPTER 2

REBUILD MY CHURCH
THE 20TH CENTURY VERSION

Msgr. McGread would never compare himself to St. Francis of Assisi. He is far too humble. However, it is interesting to note the many commonalities between the two men. Both lived with a bold faith which led them to make a tremendous impact on the Church. Both were called by the Lord to give their lives for His service. Both followed the Lord's call in a life-giving way, bringing many more people to give their own lives to the Lord. And, given those commonalities, it is particularly intriguing to note how Msgr. McGread's faith began to impact the Church in a deep way when he agreed to take the daunting assignment at the growing parish of St. Francis of Assisi.

Irony? Some might say. But looking back at all Msgr. McGread was able to accomplish there, it is clear that his assignment at St. Francis was definitely an act guided by God. The Lord obviously saw it fit to place Msgr. McGread under the patronage of this great saint as he followed in his footsteps helping to change people's hearts and minds and even their actions in an extreme way, and, through that, strengthening the Church as a whole.

It was back in the twelfth century when St. Francis heard the call. He had recently had a change of heart, deciding for himself to live solely for God. Having decided to forego his aspirations of a military career in order to put on the armor of God and fight for Him, Francis was praying in front of the crucifix at the desolate and neglected chapel of San Damiano. There, as he knelt in prayer, Francis heard a voice say to him, "Go, Francis, and repair my house, which, as you see, is falling into ruin."

St. Francis took the directive literally, and immediately he went about rebuilding the chapel of San Damiano, a church building that was literally falling down.

Following the successful rebuilding of San Damiano, Francis continued living what he believed was his call, and he rebuilt two other dilapidated churches in the area.

Then one day, while he was at Mass, Francis heard the Gospel of Matthew 10:1, 5-10 proclaimed. It was a familiar reading, but that day he heard it in a new way.

"Then he summoned his twelve disciples and gave them authority over unclean spirits to drive them out and to cure every disease and every illness. ... Jesus sent out these twelve after instructing them thus, "Do not go into pagan territory or enter a Samaritan town. Go rather to the lost sheep of the

house of Israel. As you go, make this proclamation: 'The kingdom of heaven is at hand. Cure the sick, raise the dead, cleanse lepers, drive out demons. Without cost you have received; without cost you are to give. Do not take gold or silver or copper for your belts; no sack for the journey, or a second tunic, or sandals, or walking stick..."

Francis believed this Gospel passage was speaking to him personally that day, and so, immediately following Mass, he threw away his cloak and his shoes, his walking stick, and even his empty wallet and set out to preach the Gospel. With profound fervor, he set about "rebuilding the Church" in an even greater way than he originally intended. With a renewed sense of his vocation, Francis would bring countless people through the ages to Christ.

Msgr. McGread did not hear his calling in quite the same dramatic way. He didn't hear a voice tell him to rebuild the Church. Rather, he heard Bishop Carroll tell him to build St. Anne's and then to build St. Jude's and then, after he had built a number of church buildings from the ground up, Msgr. McGread heard Bishop Maloney tell him to go to St. Francis where he would build the Church in a different, some would say even greater, way. There, Msgr. McGread would find his vocation begin to impact others as he simply did as St. Francis once did – preached the Gospel in his words and actions.

As a building, the church of St. Francis was in good condition. It was, after all, only nine years old at the time.

The walls were up, the carpet had been laid; even the pews, the baptismal font and the altar were set in place. It was a "temporary" building. But, for the time being, it was meeting the needs of the people. The parish had been established. It would seem, at first glance, that Msgr. McGread's time at St. Francis would involve much less work than his previous years as a priest had required. But, as Msgr. McGread found out shortly after arriving, that wasn't the case. Sure, the parish was established. The church building had been built, but as a parish family St. Francis was in need of rebuilding.

In fact, St. Francis parish was rapidly achieving a reputation as a priests' graveyard. Pastors couldn't handle the gravity of the situation. "I was the fourth pastor in a period of three years," notes Msgr. McGread. "I told Bishop Maloney, after he asked me to go there, that I would try it for six months and see how it went. And he agreed with me. He would let me leave if it didn't work out." But God had long-term plans that would keep Msgr. McGread as pastor of St. Francis for the next thirty-one years.

The parish was swimming in debt. Enrollment at the parish school had dropped to 200 students and was declining more each month. Discord split the parish, which was more a collection of cliques than a unified parish family. St. Francis lacked any semblance of community. "When I arrived there, you would have thought that at least 50% of the parishioners were against anything going on in the parish at all," Msgr. McGread recalls. But he soon discovered that there were only about 10 people who were heavily involved in the parish, and it was those 10 who were opposed to almost everything that the previous pastors had tried to do in the parish. Msgr. McGread soon learned that the complaints of those 10 were so disruptive that many of St. Francis' registered parishioners were attending Mass elsewhere. He realized that he had to work quickly in order to draw his parishioners back to their home parish

Immediately, he went to work preparing the parish for a new way of life, one that he hoped would strengthen them as a community and bring them all closer to Christ. However, it would not be that simple. Msgr. McGread faced an uphill battle.

He asked more parishioners to join the different parish committees, in order to give the broader parish community a real voice. Then, he worked to lead the whole parish in the ways of Christian discipleship.

"One of the first things I suggested to the parish leaders, which I had done in my prior parish assignments, was to develop Stewardship," Msgr. McGread says. He believed that Stewardship would help to unify the parish, reawaken the spiritual life of the parishioners as well as help their dire financial situation. However, the Finance Committee wouldn't hear of it. Since the parish's finances were in such terrible shape, they wanted to focus solely on ways to increase their collections. And, although that went against all that Msgr. McGread believed would serve to truly strengthen the parish, he let them proceed with their own ideas. "One of the things they decided to do," Msgr. McGread recalls, "which was popular at that time, was to publish the names of parishioners and how much money they gave in the parish bulletin. I told them that this plan was destined to be an absolute disaster, which it was." The strategy proved to simply call attention to the lack of parishioner involvement and the parish's increasing financial needs. Seeing no positive changes, the Finance Committee members' frustration grew. So, they turned to Msgr. McGread and finally agreed to give Stewardship a try. "And that's how we got things started here," Msgr. McGread says.

Armed with a vision from the words of St. Peter: "*As each one has received a gift, use it to serve one another as good stewards of God's varied grace*"- (I Peter 4:10), Msgr. McGread began leading the people of St. Francis on a life-changing Stewardship journey.

"We began our Stewardship journey at St. Francis by appealing to people with regard to their time," Msgr. McGread recalls. "Everybody has time. We all have a particular amount of time here on Earth." And that is an element of life that, Msgr. McGread believes, is too often dismissed. We need to focus on the time we have here on Earth as the gift that it is. God has given us this time, so we must use it to glorify Him. It was with this in mind that Msgr. McGread first called his parishioners to a change of heart. He challenged them to consider their time as a gift and to reflect on what they do with the time they have been given.

"How do we use this time?" he asked them. "Each of us was called by Almighty God to be a saint. As we stand before that final judgment, we will be asked what we did during our lifetime." God won't just be looking for those who did the most magnificent and outstanding things. But He will want to know how well we served Him by serving others."

Jesus Himself tells us this in the Gospel of Matthew with the parable of the judgment of the nations:

"When the Son of Man comes in his glory, and all the angels with him, he will sit upon his glorious throne, and all the nations will be assembled before him. And he will separate them one from another, as a shepherd separates the sheep from the goats. He will place the sheep on his right and the goats on his left. Then the king will say to those on his right, 'Come, you who are blessed by my Father. Inherit the kingdom prepared for you from the foundation of the world. For I was hungry and you gave me food, I was thirsty and you gave me drink, a stranger and you welcomed me, naked and you clothed me, ill and you cared for me, in prison and you visited me.' Then the righteous will answer him and say, 'Lord, when did we see you hungry and feed you, or thirsty and give you drink? When did

*we see you a stranger and welcome you, or naked
and clothe you? When did we see you ill or in prison, and visit you?' And the king will say to them in
reply, 'Amen, I say to you, whatever you did for one
of these least brothers of mine, you did for me.'
Then he will say to those on his left, 'Depart from
me, you accursed, into the eternal fire prepared for
the devil and his angels. For I was hungry and you
gave me no food, I was thirsty and you gave me no
drink, a stranger and you gave me no welcome,
naked and you gave me no clothing, ill and in prison, and you did not care for me.' Then they will answer and say, 'Lord, when did we see you hungry or
thirsty or a stranger or naked or ill or in prison,
and not minister to your needs?' He will answer
them, 'Amen, I say to you, what you did not do for
one of these least ones, you did not do for me.' And
these will go off to eternal punishment, but the
righteous to eternal life."*

(Matthew 25:31-46)

"In other words, God will want to know how we took
care of people's needs," Msgr. McGread explains. "That's
really what the Stewardship way of life does. It provides
us with the opportunity to care for one another's needs
just as Jesus has asked us to do."

Msgr. McGread encouraged his new St. Francis parish
family to examine how much time they gave to God.

"After all, we know we cannot exist without God," Msgr. McGread recognizes. "That is how dependant we are upon Almighty God. We can't move, we can't breathe without him. And yet, how much time do we really give to God each and every day of our lives?"

Following that, Msgr. McGread asked his parishioners to think about how much time they gave to serving others, beginning with those in their own families.

"How much time do husbands and wives give to each other?" he asked them. "How much time do parents give to their children?"

Msgr. McGread believes that focusing on who and what we give our time to helps us to recognize what is most important in our lives. It provides us with the opportunity to reevaluate and reprioritize. So he began inviting his parishioners to focus on their use of time during his early months at St. Francis. He soon found that his parishioners were ready for this challenge.

For the next nine months, the people of St. Francis analyzed the use of their time – both as individuals and as a parish family. Msgr. McGread used every opportunity he could to reinforce this element of Stewardship, and his parishioners seemed to be receptive to his message. They began appreciating their lives as gifts from the Lord in a whole new way, and, with that, their personal relationships with the Lord were growing stronger as well.

Meanwhile, Msgr. McGread initiated the publication of a monthly parish newsletter, which he called "The

Vernacular." The newsletter, which was left at the doors of the church for people to take home, included information about parish events and activities. It also highlighted a number of ways in which people could begin to embrace Stewardship at St. Francis. The newsletter highlighted some of the blessings parishioners could expect when they embraced stewardship, like ownership of their parish, closer ties to one another as a family, and a deeper relationship with God. Msgr. McGread believed that the more people were aware of what was happening within the parish, the more they would want to get involved.

How right he was! With the publication of "The Vernacular" and the increased awareness about parish ilfe that it offered, St. Francis of Assisi saw a big jump in parishioner involvement and, in turn, a more familial atmosphere within the parish.

Yet, it wasn't the mere publication of written material that elicited this change within the parish. In fact, the written material, though a useful and effective tool, was incredibly secondary to the leadership that Msgr. McGread showed his people. He led by example, living as a grateful steward, using his time, talent and treasure to serve the Lord and His Church. He invited his parishioners to join him on the journey. He encouraged them to take a step forward in faith and commit to a life of Stewardship. And it was with this loving leadership that the parishioners were convicted to respond.

In May 1969, nearly a year after he arrived at St. Francis, Msgr. McGread invited all adult parishioners to a free parish dinner. There, those who accepted the invitation were introduced to the concept of the Pastoral Council, a newly formed councilial concept that Vatican II required every parish to implement. Msgr. McGread intended to obey the directives of Vatican II and establish a Pastoral Council at St. Francis, but he wanted to keep his parishioners informed. You see, as far as Msgr. McGread was concerned, St. Francis was the parishioners' parish. Sure, he was their pastor and, as such, their leader, but he wanted the parishioners to know that St. Francis was theirs. He wanted them to take ownership, and he knew that keeping them informed and giving them a voice was extremely important. In addition, the dinner was to serve as a way to thank parishioners for their involvement in the parish. Yet, it wasn't as simple as that.

The idea of a *free* parish family meal was foreign to the parishioners. "We had quite a time convincing the parishioners that there was no catch to the free dinner," Msgr. McGread laughingly recalls. "But after they came to the dinner they realized there was no catch." In fact, once he got the parishioners to come, the dinner was very effective. "It really helped the parishioners to realize that the parish can be a thankful place too." Those who came to the dinner recognized that they were being invited by their loving pastor to take part in a parish family and that their participation in this family was greatly appreciated.

The dinner helped them see that each one of them was a vital part of the parish. In fact, that first dinner was so successful that the parish has continued to hold an annual parishioner appreciation dinner ever since. "We need to thank these parishioners for what they do," Msgr. McGread says. "You can never be thankful enough, because that's what the Stewardship way of life is all about."

Finally, just a year after Msgr. McGread's arrival, life at St. Francis was beginning to change in some very positive ways.

"The people were becoming much more friendly, with me and with one another," Msgr. McGread recalls. "They were becoming a parish family, and that was encouraging for me to see. It seemed as if the 'cliques' that had basically run the parish were becoming more a part of the whole parish family and everyone together was growing to love their parish, growing to love the Church, and growing closer to Christ."

Seeing parishioners grow in their relationships with Christ excited Msgr. McGread and reinvigorated his own faith and his commitment to the Stewardship way of life.

"All I wanted to do was to bring the parishioners closer to Christ. I wanted to unite them to one another and to the Lord, and seeing that, through Stewardship, God was allowing this to happen was overwhelming."

That's not to say that Msgr. McGread did not run into any problems at the parish. There were, indeed, some parishioners who were strongly opposed to living the Stewardship way of life.

"I find that generally at all parishes about one-third of the parishioners do not want to follow the leadership of the pastor," Msgr. McGread relates. "It seems there is always that one-third who is determined to be defiant. But you cannot allow them to dishearten you or weaken your resolve. As pastors we are called to lead them all to Christ, and we must continually do so even when we see some resisting."

With that in mind, Msgr. McGread continued encouraging all his parishioners to embrace the Stewardship way of life at St. Francis. He continued publishing monthly newsletters, informing the parishioners about what was going on in the parish – what ministries were available, what events were taking place – and encouraging them to participate. He also continued to preach heavily on Stewardship. His homilies were heartfelt and powerful. He had the gift of weaving the message of Stewardship into all of his homilies, and he did so not in a "screaming Stewardship from the pulpit" sort of a way, but in a subtle way that quite effectively spoke to the hearts of his people. In preaching the Gospel, Msgr. McGread was preaching Stewardship. He recognized that they go hand-in-hand, and his homilies helped the parishioners recognize that too.

"There is something very attractive about the way Msgr. McGread lives his life and the way he preaches," explains Dan Loughman, a St. Francis parishioner who served as a member of the original Stewardship Committee. "People were drawn to him – they still are – because he is completely genuine. He truly cares for people. He wants to bring people to Christ, so people want to listen to him, they want to follow his lead."

St. Francis parishioners watched as Msgr. McGread set an example, not only preaching Stewardship with his words, but by the life he lived. He offered his time to the Lord in prayer. He attended many ministry meetings and often cooked food for the other participants to enjoy. And he offered the first fruits of his finances back to the Lord. The parishioners saw their pastor practicing what he preached, and they were eager to follow suit.

Every year, Msgr. McGread invited his parishioners to make a commitment to Stewardship in writing. He published materials detailing the specifics of the different parish ministries and giving the parishioners an opportunity to commit to get involved and to commit time to the Lord in prayer. Year after year, he asked them to renew their commitment during their annual Stewardship Renewal.

"When they put it into writing, people are more apt to follow through on their commitments," Msgr. McGread acknowledges.

Then, in the 1980s, Msgr. McGread extended yet another invitation to his parishioners. He asked a core group of parishioners to join him in leading this Stewardship venture. They were men and women whom Msgr. McGread could see were grasping the concept of Stewardship and, even more, taking it to heart. They were the parish's first Stewardship Committee.

Up to that point, he was doing things on his own, with the help of a few volunteers, and the Stewardship Committee would provide him and the parish with much needed support on this parish journey.

"We're not really sure why he picked us," Dan Loughman admits. "All twelve of us were on this journey of Stewardship. There was some spark of conversion in our hearts and minds. He must have sensed that."

He asked the committee to get a sense of the needs of this parish – to play kind of a support-role to the Pastoral Council, which was already in place. That Pastoral Council was well structured and doing their job quite successfully, but the parish was growing rapidly and the demographics were changing. Msgr. McGread wanted to be sure that he was meeting the needs of his parishioners and properly ministering to them. His hope was that the Stewardship Committee would provide him with additional advice and support as he ministered to the growing parish.

The Stewardship Committee began to meet on a weekly basis. They would pray together, bond with one another, and share their insights – all while Msgr. McGread was sitting in as a member of the committee himself. He would listen to the members' ideas and suggestions and then he would throw in his own. It was a think-tank, recognizing and discussing parish needs. Yet, at the same time, the Stewardship Committee was more than just a formal committee, they were becoming a family. Their own bonds with one another strengthened as they met together and then their commitment to really serve the parish grew as well.

Msgr. McGread invited the Stewardship Committee to continue developing the annual Stewardship Renewal process. He wanted them to refine the process and make it something that they thought would function effectively. That's when the first real thorough review of the time and talent forms that St. Francis was using for their renewals took place. The committee reviewed the design and the content of the forms and then they took it a step further, designing treasure forms for the next renewal.

Slowly but surely, parishioner after parishioner responded to the call. They were getting involved in the life of their parish, strengthening their connections with one another and the parish of St. Francis was growing into a close spiritual family.

Attendance at Mass skyrocketed, involvement in parish ministries increased, and the parish's weekly offertory grew. On the whole, though, the most important thing that happened at St. Francis was not any of these three things. Rather, what happened in the hearts of the people while they honored their commitments to Stewardship changed the parish family as a whole. They were giving of themselves and loving the benefits of living this way.

At about that same time, Msgr. McGread and his parish leaders took an extremely bold step. They did away with tuition at St. Francis School. That was a particularly risky step, because, again, the school's enrollment was minimal at best, and so, therefore, were the finances. Yet, Msgr. McGread believed that a no-tuition school was necessary, and he got his leaders on board. He met with the members of the Finance Committee, and his reasoning seemed pure and simple. Parishioners should be offered Catholic education as a ministry of the parish, and they needed to trust that God would provide the necessary finances to run such a ministry. And so they did.

"We made both the elementary school and the high school available to all of the parents," Msgr. McGread recalls. "I was always very sympathetic with parents because so often you heard the story that only wealthy people could afford Catholic school. I wanted to get rid of that whole idea. To me, the school was an integral part of the parish, a mission of the parish, the same as everything else. Therefore, we all had an obligation to support whatever missions the parish had."

Bold as it was, the decision to recognize the school as a ministry of the parish and to offer it, as a ministry, with no-tuition to involved parishioners was a huge success. In fact, it was such a successful decision, that this ministry has endured for almost 40 years now. Parishioners still commit to live a Stewardship way of life, and they are still offered Catholic education at no cost. But it's not as though it's a bribe from the pastor or even, for that matter, a reward that the pastor gives them for helping the parish. Rather, the school truly serves as a ministry of the parish and, because parishioners have become so committed to Stewardship, the parish is able to completely fund the school.

What's more, as a ministry of the parish, the school forms their young people as disciples of Christ, raising up more faithful stewards for the Church!

When annual Stewardship Renewals are held each November, all of the school teachers and the parish school of religion catechists receive copies of the parish's Stewardship materials to work into their lesson plans throughout the month, enabling them to form the children in the Stewardship way of life early on. The children are seen as an important part of the parish family, and they too are encouraged to participate in each annual renewal.

"We start in the elementary school," says Msgr. McGread. "The children actually sign a form promising that they are going to be stewards. The form asks them to commit, number one, to going to church on Sunday and also to commit to serve others. It does not necessarily mean they are going to give any money," Msgr. McGread adds. "That's not the key. The big thing is that they are going to go to church on Sunday and going to do something out of service. All of them can do this. So you give them these opportunities. This is why we have some wonderful results with these kids in school."

A few years after Msgr. McGread implemented no-tuition enrollment at the school, while the Stewardship way of life was taking root, he decided to take yet another big step on the Stewardship journey with his parishioners. He conducted the first parish survey at St. Francis, giving the parishioners a real voice.

"I wanted to find out what the parishioners were interested in, what their needs were," he says. "It was kind of reverse psychology. Instead of being told what they should be interested in, I wanted my parishioners to tell me what they needed, and what they wanted from the parish."

Even though he was not sure what his parishioners would say, Msgr. McGread took the chance, because he wanted to meet their needs. He also wanted to help them take ownership in the parish. He wanted to make it very clear that this was, indeed, their parish, and that he was committed to caring for them. So, he published the survey's findings. People's names were not included, but the many wants and needs that had been identified were shared with the entire parish.

Msgr. McGread and his leaders gathered very valuable information from these surveys, and they used what they learned from their fellow parishioners to help direct the growth of parish programs, facilities, and activities in the years that followed.

After sowing the seeds of Stewardship at St. Francis for many years, Msgr. McGread was seeing it take root in the hearts of his people, and the changes in the parish were undeniable. "Our collections were noticeably large," Msgr. McGread says. "And this is what began to appeal to a number of people throughout this country." The changes at St. Francis appealed to so many, in fact, that parishes and dioceses around the nation asked him to come speak about what he had done. "But whenever I went to talk to dioceses about Stewardship I told them that the collection money was not the successful story of St. Francis," Msgr. McGread recalls. "The successful story of St. Francis was the involvement of our people."

Msgr. McGread is quick to point out that the vision of time, talent and treasure being the tenets of the Steward-ship way of life is biblically based. As such, Stewardship is not a fundraising program. Rather, Stewardship is a spiritual way of life. "Once we adopt a Stewardship way of life, we are in it for the duration, we are in it for life," Msgr. McGread says.

True Christian stewardship is not relegated to one aspect of a disciple's life. Rather, it involves the whole of the person, and, therefore, the steward is invited to give of himself both within the parish and in the broader community.

As the parish involvement grew, so did the need for parish buildings. Msgr. McGread oversaw an addition to the convent, the construction of a multi-purpose building and the building of a brand new church. Within five more years, a new convent was purchased and an activities center and school were built from the ground up. A Perpetual Adoration Chapel was opened at the parish in 1986 and made available twenty-four hours a day, seven days a week (except during the hours of Sunday Mass).

In the meantime, Msgr. McGread watched as his once small parish of 600 families in 1968 expanded to 2,500 families by the mid-1980's, with nearly 800 students attending its school, and an increase in the parish offertory to $87,000 per week. The parish also expanded its service to the wider community during this time. St. Francis supported three non-parish schools in Wichita (a poor school on the south end, an African-American school, and a Latino school). "We did all this in addition to supporting a bishop in the Philippines and some missionaries in Venezuela," Msgr. McGread remarks. "And we did it all through Stewardship."

The people of St. Francis were beginning to recognize that, and, just a decade after Msgr. McGread's arrival, the broader Wichita community felt the impact of Stewardship.

One particular parishioner, Dr. Dan Tatpati, approached Msgr. McGread on his own accord. He saw that he had a gift, and he wanted to use it to serve others.

Dr. Tatpati was worried about the children of uninsured parents not getting their shots. He wanted to open a free clinic at St. Francis. Msgr. McGread was more than willing to help open the clinic, and he was thrilled to see his parishioner taking such initiative. Yet, he also knew that St. Francis wasn't the place to do it.

"The families in need are downtown," Msgr. McGread remembers explaining. "I told him we would try to secure a facility downtown and open the clinic there."

And so they did. Msgr. McGread approached Bishop Eugene Gerber, then-bishop of Wichita, and asked him if he knew of a place downtown where the clinic could be established. Bishop Gerber led them to a school in downtown Wichita that had been closed. There, Dr. Tatpati began offering free shots, and it wasn't long before numerous doctors and nurses were volunteering their time and talents to this ministry. That first month, the group of health professionals cared for about 50 patients. Today, in the Guadalupe Clinic, they see up-wards of 50 patients a day – children and adults. Patients simply walk in and receive care. If people are in need, they are cared for. Yet the doctors and nurses who serve in the clinic (which now functions under the umbrella of the Diocese of Wichita) feel as though they are the privileged ones. They are blessed to care for those in need.

Msgr. McGread is convinced that parishioners have responded so well because the parish has always been concerned with meeting people's needs, and providing them with opportunities to serve one another. "We all have the tendency to really help in emergencies," he says.

"If there is a death in your area what do most of the neighbors do? They bake food and they go to the house. That's the goodness that exists in all of us. The Steward-ship way of life will provide us with opportunities for that goodness, not only on the occasion of a tragedy, but every day of our lives. That is the difference. So Steward-ship gives us all these opportunities really to do some-thing for one another." And once the parishioners became aware of the numerous opportunities and were encouraged to serve one another in a new way, they responded with gusto!

It is true for every parish family – as the years go by, things change. Pastors are reassigned. Parish demographics are different. These and many other such changes can make it hard for a parish to continue living Stewardship in the manner that they have been. Over the years, St. Francis has experienced such changes. They've seen three pastors since Msgr. McGread, and two other parishes have been established near St. Francis. While they have been blessed with pastors who have worked to continue living the Stewardship way of life and guiding the people in that way, some parishioners have moved to one of the new parishes. That has greatly changed the demographics at St. Francis. There are not as many young families, many of the parishioners are older and retired. These changes have presented some challenges. They have contributed to lower offertory collections week-to-week and different ministry involvement. Yet, Stewardship continues to be lived out, and the St. Francis parishioners stress that Stewardship can and should be lived even amidst great change in the parish. However, continual Stewardship formation is vital.

"There must be on-going Stewardship education and formation from the pulpit, through the newsletter, and generally from parishioner to parishioner," Dan Loughman explains. "That's the only way that Stewardship can continue."

What's more, he says that pastors and parishioners alike need to be aware that when the demographics of a parish change, the "look" of Stewardship will change as well. There may not be as much money in the basket every week. There may not be the same types of ministries at the parish. That's okay. In fact, that's necessary. What's important is that the pastor is working to serve the needs of the parish and bringing them closer to Christ through constant invitation, education, and formation.

A VIEW FROM THE PEW:
STEWARDSHIP CHANGES LIVES

Paul and Bettie Eck were some of the earliest members of St. Francis parish. They joined in 1960, only a few months after the parish's founding. Yet they were not heavily involved – not initially anyway.

"There were a few people who did everything, and they wanted it that way," Bettie remembers.

As a result, Bettie and Paul were hesitant to get involved. Rather, they just sat back and watched things take place. It wasn't as though they had no desire to get involved. In fact, they had children in the religious education program and in the school, and they were eager to play a role in those two ministries. But the atmosphere of the parish was not conducive to their involvement.

"We did not feel welcomed," Bettie remembers.

Then, in 1968, Msgr. McGread was appointed pastor, and life completely changed for Bettie and Paul and so many others at St. Francis.

"He has such a hospitable personality," Bettie explains. "With him at the helm, you just felt welcomed. He made you feel like you belonged, and that made it much easier to want to get involved."

What's more, Msgr. McGread preached about Stewardship from the get-go, inviting all of his parishioners to offer their gifts of time, talent and treasure.

"With a new sense of belonging, the Stewardship message really hit home," Bettie remembers. "Of course, for me, it wasn't too hard a message to grasp. I had grown up a Southern Baptist, and being involved in church and tithing was something we always did. Yet, Msgr. McGread's approach to it all helped us understand the deeper meaning behind giving of ourselves. He helped us to see that it wasn't just about giving because the parish needed our time, talent, and treasure to survive, but rather, that we had a need to give in order to thank the Lord for all He's done."

Bettie, still quite a shy person, found small ways to give of her time and talent, including serving the school lunch program.

Paul, meanwhile, was armed with great financial expertise, and, though he admits that giving his time and talent was not incredibly easy for him at first, he stepped outside of his comfort zone and got involved.

"I have to give a lot of credit to Msgr. McGread and the Holy Spirit," Paul says. "The Holy Spirit had to be working over time with people like me to convince. I was a very bashful person, so getting involved wasn't something I jumped at. But Msgr. McGread encouraged me. He has a way of drawing people in, of helping people see that they do have great gifts and that their gifts are important for the parish."

Paul served as a member of the Finance Committee and the Parish Council in those early days. In addition, together, Paul and Bettie served as members of the first Stewardship Committee at St. Francis, an experience that changed them forever.

"We grew in our understanding of what it means to be a steward as members of that committee," Paul says. "We also strengthened our relationships with some of our fellow parishioners, connecting with other committee members during the regular meetings. It was an experience that drew us much closer to Christ as we understood our call to discipleship and closer to one another as we strived to live that call together."

Then, came the time for the Ecks to take yet another step forward in faith and offer their gifts of treasure. Paul chuckles at the thought of that decision now, because he says it wasn't an entirely faith-filled decision for him. At that time, Msgr. McGread encouraged all parish families to offer 5% of their income as tithe to the parish and 2% to the diocese or other charities. So, Paul and Bettie simply followed Msgr. McGread's lead and did what he encouraged them to do.

"Initially, my decision to tithe was not fueled by a belief in my need to give," Paul admits.

Yet as Paul and Bettie continued to give of themselves – their time, their talents, and their treasure – they began to realize the wisdom in Msgr. McGread's guidance and encouragement. They began to realize that they, as Christian disciples, had a need to give of themselves and that the more they gave of themselves, the more they received in return. God was blessing them – far beyond their expectations.

"We grew stronger as Catholics and as a married couple," Bettie says. "In fact, today, as we continue to live out the Stewardship way of life, we continue to grow in our faith. It is a never-ending journey. It is a wonderful journey. It has completely changed us, and we owe a huge debt of gratitude to Msgr. McGread for his wonderful example."

For his part, Paul assures us, "Once you start to truly live the Stewardship way of life – to acknowledge the gifts God has given you and to give them back in gratitude to God – you will never be the same. Stewardship has changed my outlook on life. It has made me a much more grateful person. It has made me a much more faith-filled person. And, today, as I see my children living it out with their families, I am in awe. It is wonderful to see your children living as Christ's disciples and raising their own children to do the same. The blessings of Stewardship are, indeed, overflowing."

Msgr. McGread as a young priest

Msgr. McGread & his sister, Gerti, and her family

Kathleen McGread, Msgr. McGread's sister

Msgr. McGread and sisters Theresa & Kathleen

*Msgr. McGread celebrating Mass at
his 25th anniversary celebration*

*Msgr. McGread celebrating Mass at
his 25th anniversary celebration*

Msgr. McGread's 25th anniversary celebration

Msgr. McGread's 25th anniversary celebration

*Msgr. McGread at his 25ᵗʰ anniversary
celebration with his brother, Pat*

*1974 Groundbreaking for St. Francis Church – L to R: Tom
Sanders, architect, Fr. Tom, Bishop Moloney, Jerry Simpson &
unknown*

2005 Reunion of original stewardship committee –
L to R: Ernie & Jean Renfri/ Jim & Dorothy Downing/
Paul & Bettie Eck/ Dale & Alice Wiggins/ Jim & Margarite
Weinmann/ Dan & Carolyn Laughman

CHAPTER 3

THE ROOTS OF STEWARDSHIP BEGIN TO SPREAD

From St. Francis Parish to the Diocese of Wichita

As Stewardship was flourishing on the parish level at St. Francis of Assisi, great things were beginning to happen on the diocesan level as well. God was at work, and, as the new chief shepherd of the diocese, Bishop Gerber was open and willing to do his part.

Much like Msgr. McGread, when Bishop Gerber arrived on the scene, he wanted to ensure that his ministry was meeting the needs of the people. What's more, he knew that what his people needed more than anything was to grow closer to Christ and to serve Him by serving His people.

Two years prior to Bishop Gerber's arrival, his predecessor, Bishop David Maloney, had Msgr. McGread and a few other priests put together a plan for an annual diocesan appeal.

For some reason, known only to the Holy Spirit, the plan was never implemented. "We gave it to him," Msgr. McGread says. "And then it sat on his desk for the next two years. Then he retired."

So, after Bishop Gerber was installed, in 1983, he read through the plan and consulted with others individually and in groups and decided to structure two parallel initiatives in order to develop a diocesan pastoral plan.

- The first one was called "Emmaus" and it was directed toward the priests of the diocese with two goals: 1) to assist each priest in his own spiritual renewal, and 2) to aid the priests along with their bishop in a renewal of their communal spirituality and in their awareness of mission.

- The second one was called "A People Gathered" and it was directed to pastors and key leaders in each parish throughout the diocese. The bishop asked them to come together and prayerfully ponder three questions: 1) what are the qualities of a vibrant parish, 2) what are the obstacles to becoming a vibrant parish, and 3) what would you do if you had unlimited resources.

The bishop then gathered the people together on the parish level, the deanery level and then the diocesan level and discussed the three questions. In an effort to address and meet the needs and desires that the people identified, Bishop Gerber put together a diocesan pastoral plan.

One key component of that plan was an initiative that the bishop named United Catholic Stewardship (UCS). Through UCS, which involved individuals committing to put their gifts at the service of one another and parishes holding annual Stewardship Renewals and more, the diocese began living the Stewardship way of life together. The fire of Stewardship that had been burning in the hearts of the people of St. Francis of Assisi was now sending sparks across the entire Diocese of Wichita.

A diocesan Office of Stewardship was put in place to help parishes implement the essential elements of UCS, and a number of priests and lay people were identified and asked to help individual parish leadership groups with the implementation. Notably helpful were Msgr. McGread and a number of lay people from St. Francis of Assisi, who had fruitfully been living Stewardship for many years.

In addition to the launching of UCS, the people of the diocese called for a new retreat center and a priests' retirement home. Everyone throughout the diocese was invited to contribute to the building and staffing of these facilities and to increase the diocese's funds for sustaining retired priests. To this end, all who participated pledged $17,500,000 – over and above their financial commitments to their parishes.

It was then decided that they would add a Catholic Memory Care Center with the funds coming from industrial revenue bonds. And yet, the diocese's projects didn't end there. Since then, they have added an assisted living home, a memory care home, and an independent living home called Shepherd's Crossing to the grounds of the campus.

The retreat center, which is housed on the same campus but separated a bit from these other facilities by a beautiful lake is called the Spiritual Life Center. Its mission is to offer adult education, leadership development, spiritual formation, and family enrichment. In the last several years, the Spiritual Life Center has welcomed some 16,000 people annually to participate in their programs and experience true Christian hospitality.

Both Bishop Gerber and Msgr. McGread, as well as the diocese as a whole, were in awe. They were seeing the amazing results of people embracing the Stewardship way of life. They could now meet the needs of their people in an even better way than they had imagined, all because the good people of the Diocese of Wichita responded in gratitude to God through the living of Stewardship as their way of life.

The people of the diocese began living their faith with greater fervor, responding to the needs they saw within their parishes and within their greater communities. In fact, they responded so generously that even when a large need was noticed, the response was immediate and overwhelming. The people of the Diocese of Wichita had committed on a broad scale to be Christ's disciples, and they would serve Him as such – in and out of their parish boundaries.

In one such instance, Bishop Gerber recognized that while there were places throughout the city where the poor could receive shelter and even meals in the daytime, there was nowhere for them to eat a warm meal at night. He had a deep desire to care for the poor, and he wanted to provide them with that nightly meal. He wanted to meet that need, and he felt sure that the generous people of his diocese would heed the call. Yet what happened even blew him away. The people not only gave of their finances for the project, with the hearts of true stewards they offered their own time and talent as well.

Bishop Gerber gathered 17 contractors and sub-contractors, presented his hopes to them, received their reactions and asked what they could do at-cost, below-cost, or at no cost. These and other contractors – Catholic and non-Catholic – joined in the effort, eager to see the bishop's vision come to fruition. By the time the facility was completed, it opened its doors, offering the first meal without any money due.

The facility, which Bishop Gerber named The Lord's Diner in recognition of the Lord's hand at work in it all, now serves about 500 men, women and children every day. Some 6,000 volunteers from a number of different faith communities and a small staff make this possible. There is one shift of volunteers in the afternoon who work to prepare the food and another shift in the evening when volunteers serve, wash dishes and clean up.

In yet another effort to encourage them to live Stewardship as a way of life, United Catholic Stewardship invited the entire diocesan family to take responsibility for the education and religious formation of the youth. To this end, the elementary Catholic education was initially offered without tuition throughout the diocese – following the example of St. Francis of Assisi parish. Then, years later, the diocese was able to offer that same educational opportunity to high school students as well.

Today, some 11,000 students throughout the Diocese of Wichita receive Catholic education without tuition. Some rural elementary schools have re-opened, others added back upper grades that had been dropped and new substantial additions have been made to parish elementary and diocesan high schools in an effort to accommodate the increasing number of students whose parents want their children to receive a Catholic education.

"All of this has been accomplished because people want to practice Stewardship," Msgr. McGread assures us as he reflects on the numerous ways through the years that the people of Wichita have chosen to live their lives as Christ's disciples.

It really is a spiritual experience. The choice to live the Stewardship way of life begins by a conversion of heart. Parishioners are invited to encounter Christ, to see all that He has done for them and to offer Him their lives in gratitude by serving one another. True Christian Stewardship is, in fact, simply living as a disciple of Christ, following Jesus' example and serving one another all for the glory of God! And today, the people of Wichita are undoubtedly encountering Christ as they serve one another and, in that, they are growing closer to Him. They are active in their parishes and in the greater community. They are attending Mass regularly like never before, and they are eager to spread the good news about what God has done for them, encouraging more people to respond to God's gifts in generosity.

When they began promoting Stewardship on the diocesan level in 1985, approximately 60% of all registered Catholics in the diocese were attending Mass on a weekly basis. Now, more than 78% of them do. On top of that, their elementary and high schools are now not only updated, but they are funded entirely by the gifts of generous parishioners, offering all active parishioners throughout the diocese an opportunity to send their children to a Catholic school as part of the mission of their parish. Retired priests now have beautiful apartments in which they reside, thanks to the generosity of those living the Stewardship way of life. And the list goes on and on. It would be impossible to fully explain the innumerable ways in which the Stewardship people within the Diocese of Wichita are currently serving one another. It really is awe-inspiring. Yet, what Msgr. McGread and, surely, the whole diocese would want us all to know is that they have been able to do all of this because

God is good. It is not because their diocese is unique in some way or their parishioners are rich and talented beyond measure. They are ordinary Catholics living the wonderful life that God invites all of us to live. All of this is possible because the people have responded to God's invitation to practice Stewardship as the response of a disciple. They have chosen to live their lives in service to Him, and the fruits can be clearly seen.

"Stewardship is responsible for all of this," Msgr. McGread assures us. And what that means is that, what the Diocese of Wichita has so wonderfully been able to accomplish, is possible elsewhere, even, perhaps, everywhere. In Msgr. McGread's eyes, it's not even about following Wichita's example. Rather, living Stewardship involves following Jesus' lead. And that is what Stewardship is all about!

"Some people say I started Stewardship," Msgr. McGread acknowledges while grasping his Bible. But he doesn't make this claim. "It's all there," he says as he points to the Bible in his hand. "I did not start Stewardship. Christ started Stewardship."

But what Msgr. McGread and the people of the Diocese of Wichita as a whole did do was say yes to God. They have given their lives to the Lord and in so doing, they offer us an example, a modern-day example, that we can follow in our own parishes and dioceses.

Caution: No-Tuition Schools

There are potential pitfalls for any Catholic parish considering offering education without tuition. These include staying in conformity with the laws and regulations of the Internal Revenue Service (IRS).

The first and most important action to take as you consider going to no-tuition is to get professional counsel from a tax attorney or a certified public accountant who is versed in this area of tax law. This attorney or CPA needs to be familiar with the applicable tax law and your parish's unique situation, not only at the outset but in an ongoing way in case of changes in the law or changes in the parish's situation that could result in potential problems.

The second thing to do is to obtain a copy of the IRS Revenue Ruling 83-104 and become familiar with the key provisions in that ruling.

From the Diocese to the Nation – Msgr. McGread influences the US Bishops' Pastoral Letter

It wasn't just Bishop Gerber who took note of all Msgr. McGread had done at St. Francis and the incredible impact that Stewardship had there. The United States Bishops as a whole took notice, and, as the Stewardship way of life continued to change the hearts and the minds and the lives of the people at St. Francis and throughout the Diocese of Wichita, the US Conference of Catholic Bishops recognized the need to encourage the whole nation to live Stewardship. And so began the work on their pastoral letter, *Stewardship: A Disciple's Response*.

Msgr. McGread recalls his involvement in the development of the pastoral letter.

"Work on the bishops' Pastoral Letter began in 1990," he says. "It came about because some of the bishops realized how important the Stewardship way of life really was in properly forming a parish community, and they saw how it had worked in different parts of the country. There were several different versions of Stewardship (some centered primarily on the treasure element), but the bishops were interested in communicating the real meaning of Stewardship through their work."

One thing they knew for sure was that their treatment of Stewardship would not focus on fundraising efforts, but rather it would be centered on the Bible and the Eucharist. They wanted to form Christ-centered disciples who would give their lives to God's service.

At the time, Archbishop Thomas Murphy of Seattle was serving as the head of the Ad Hoc Committee on Stewardship – the USCCB group that was working on writing a pastoral letter about Stewardship. And it was amidst the writing process that the archbishop met up with Msgr. McGread at a National Stewardship Conference. The two became good friends, and Archbishop Murphy asked Msgr. McGread to get involved. He knew that Msgr. McGread was a great example of discipleship lived through Stewardship and, on top of that, he had successfully educated his parishioners in the Christo-centric ways of true Stewardship. And Msgr. McGread willingly offered his service.

"Initially the bishops didn't want to call it Steward-ship because to them, Stewardship meant money, which it means to an awful lot of people," Msgr. McGread remembers. "But we convinced them that Stewardship actually was a Biblical word. Nineteen of the major parables in the Bible relate directly to Stewardship. And the bishops agreed that they needed to explain what being a steward really is from the point of view of Christ in the Bible."

What does that entail? "Being a steward really means being a manager," Msgr. McGread explains. As stewards, we are managing the gifts God gave to us. We are charged to manage the gifts God has given in order to help spread the Kingdom of God on this Earth, to help others come to know the Lord.

Recall the parable of the talents - Matthew 25:14-29.

The U.S. bishops wanted the whole nation to under-stand this concept.

As the bishops continued their work on the pastoral letter, they asked Msgr. McGread to have some St. Francis parishioners write about what Stewardship meant to them. Msgr. McGread and some of his parishioners wrote letters to the bishops, illustrating how Stewardship had changed their lives. And the bishops took their personal experiences into account as they continued their work,

adding into the draft itself some of the Wichita parishioners' own words.

Then, as the bishops compiled draft after draft, Msgr.
McGread was asked to review and comment on each one
of them.

"I got copies of the drafts from Bishop Gerber in order to add things or correct things in it," he remembers.
Stewardship: A Disciple's Response was eventually published in 1992, a work of the U.S. bishops that bears a
great deal of Msgr. McGread's own experience and
expertise. Msgr. McGread is glad to see Stewardship
properly explained as "a disciple's way of life" as the title
of the Pastoral Letter denotes. Yet, unfortunately, the
letter isn't promulgated too well throughout the country.
Stewardship is still often mistaken as a program, and so
people pass over the short well-written treasure that the
bishops have given us. As Msgr. McGread says, the
pastoral letter has the capability to dispel a lot of misconception, to educate people in the ways of Stewardship
and to ultimately change our hearts and minds about
living discipleship today.

Msgr. McGread feels honored to have participated in
the publication of the bishops' letter, and he encourages
every Catholic to read it and take its message to heart.

CHAPTER 4

PRACTICAL ADVICE FOR PASTORS

While Christ calls every one of us to a life of Steward-ship, a life of true discipleship, this way of life is far from an easy one. It is not as though we answer Christ's call and everything falls into place. Truth be told, there are bound to be many trials that befall us as we strive to live Christian discipleship in this day and age. We are, after all, going against the grain of a secular society. Our efforts will be discouraged. Many people will decline the invita-tion to live Stewardship. And it may take years before we see the tangible fruits of our labor. But we cannot let those things dampen our spirits. We must have faith, put our trust in the good God we serve and press on, seeking always to be His faithful disciples and to call others to His service.

Parish pastors face a particularly challenging role in the Stewardship way of life. They are charged with the task of leading parishioners, and of transforming parish-es. In many cases, the recognized success or failure of this way of life within their parishes reflects largely on them. But it can, at the same time, be the most rewarding role to play in the life of a Stewardship parish. As pastors lead their parishioners by example, they are bound to witness the change in the hearts of their people, which, in turn, can strengthen their own Stewardship journeys.

But how do pastors proceed? What does it take to successfully implement the Stewardship way of life in the parish so that the challenges and roadblocks are minimal and the results are astounding?

"A pastor needs to understand Stewardship as a spiritual awakening within his own parish, his own community and his own life," Msgr. McGread says. "This is a way of life. It is not a program. It is a process that people need to be educated into."

At the same time, Msgr. McGread is aware that encouraging pastors to take a step further on their Stewardship journey is not always easy. Many of them are afraid to establish Stewardship as a way of life within their parishes because they are afraid of failure. Yet, as Msgr. McGread reminds us, the Stewardship way of life begins with invitation. When you invite your parishioners to be a part of this, invite them to follow Christ today, there is no failure.

"It is up to the people to respond, but that is their decision," Msgr. McGread assures us.

And they will respond. It may take some longer than others, and there are bound to be a small number of people who will not respond to the invitation. But if you extend the invitation: "Come, follow Christ with me. Give of yourselves, for the Lord has given super abundantly to you," you will find that many of your parishioners have a conversion of heart. They will respond to this invitation. And when they do, you have to allow them to take responsibility within the parish.

"Let them work at what they've volunteered to do – give them that opportunity. Empower the people in this way," Msgr. McGread encourages. "Pastors don't have to be in charge of every little iota of parish life. In fact, if a pastor is in charge of the parish's spirituality, then he's busy enough."

A pastor is indeed vital to every area of the parish's life. After all, as Msgr. McGread puts it, "nothing in the parish will happen without the pastor." But that does not mean that pastors must be in charge of executing every task or establishing every parish ministry. In fact, Msgr. McGread believes that when pastors allow their parish-ioners to take responsibility in this regard, the parishion-ers gain a sense of ownership of the parish, and, in turn, the life of the parish is rejuvenated.

Msgr. McGread recognizes that many pastors are afraid of Stewardship because of the misconception that the concept just entails extra work for the pastor. He assures us that with the help of faithful parishioners, the work will not fall solely on the pastor. In fact, he says, "If you have a good Stewardship Committee, they are the ones that do practically 99% of the work. The pastor is really the one to support them in what they are doing and to guide them. The obligation (of the priest) is to try to bring the people closer to Almighty God, because the closer you bring them to Almighty God, then the happiness comes in, because that is God's way of really preparing us for our journey to eternity. We must have that relationship in regard to God. And the Stewardship way of life will really bring us to that relationship, because we will put God first in everything we do no matter what it is. And once we realize that God is with us, then it really does not matter whether we are at work, prayer or play. If God is with us we can accomplish all sorts of things which you couldn't imagine we'd be able to accomplish. St. Paul says 'When God is with us, nothing can stand in our way.'"

Stewardship is a completely spiritual way of life. We are striving for one thing and one thing only: to follow Christ. This is what really will appeal to people about the Stewardship way of life. This is how pastors are able to reach the parishioners. Emphasize Christ! "And use the Bible," Msgr. McGread instructs. "Whenever you use the Bible, you are telling people this is what Christ wants you to do. So it's not an individual telling people what his opinion is, but rather it is Christ's opinion. And we all want to follow Christ.

"If a pastor was sitting before me today and asking the question of how he would begin Stewardship, the <u>first thing</u> I would tell him is that this is not a program, that this is a way of life. And there is quite a difference," Msgr. McGread says. "This (Stewardship) is not a program that is hit and miss – you do for one time and it is all over with. No, Stewardship is a way of life that is adopted by him (the pastor) and his parishioners through the means of invitation. And then I would ask him the question: Why did you really want to start this? And if his answer was, 'Well, we need the money,' I would correct him very quickly about that, because a Stewardship way of life is not mainly about money. It is really about bringing people closer to God. The money element comes along with that. But it is not the main emphasis. There are, indeed, three elements that are vital to the Stewardship way of life: time and talent and treasure. The important thing is not how much money the parish needs and how much Stewardship will allow the parish to raise but, rather, how we use these three elements for God and how important God is in each one of our lives. We are all God's children. He loves us every moment of our lives, and we depend upon Him for every moment we are here. So it is very important that we try to bring the people (our parishioners) into that full association with Almighty God.

"The <u>second thing</u> I would tell him is to make sure to establish a Stewardship Committee. A Stewardship Committee is very, very important to implementing the Stewardship way of life. They are the people who are going to carry out an awful lot of the work that is involved – not only in organizing the parish, but also doing the mailing and all that necessary stuff.

"And the <u>third thing</u> I would tell him is you need to find out what your needs are in your particular parish family. Every parish has several different needs, and it is very important that these needs come from your parishioners. They will be much more apt to address or meet the needs of the parish when they know that they are the ones who identified them, they are the ones who recognize that there are needs, and it's not coming from the "top" as it were.

"That is how I would advise pastors to begin, and, in a particular way, again, I would encourage pastors to deemphasize the treasure element of Stewardship until they have established the role of how people use their time and their talent. When you do that, you will find that the people realize that each of us have a personal obligation to build up a relationship with Almighty God. You will find that the Church is very important to them, because it is as a part of the Church that we experience Christ, particularly in the Eucharist and the other Sacraments. Once they establish that, they will find a sense of belonging to the Church, a sense of ownership, and then a sense of responsibility. One thing follows the other."

Yet, even when pastors educate themselves in the ways of Stewardship and then approach Stewardship in their parishes with the right intentions, not all parishioners will embrace this way of life.

"There are three different classes in the parish," says Msgr. McGread. "One third of the parishioners are wonderful good people who want to give of themselves. You have another third in the middle and then you have a third of people who have no interest in Stewardship properly lived out. As I travel throughout the country and I hear people asking, 'What can we do with them (the third that does not help out)?' my suggestion is, 'Pray for them.' That is all you can do for them. Yet, some insist, 'If we could even get a little bit of money from (this group), we could do so much more.' Forget it. When we started Stewardship at St. Francis, we had that initial 30% that went for it right away. Gradually the middle percent went for it. And then gradually even some of those in the last group went for it. But remember, that took time.

Msgr. McGread directs us: "Don't worry about your numbers. Worry about the people you can get (involved) and really take care of them. That is what is important."

In fact, Msgr. McGread remembers giving that same word of advice to the Stewardship Committee chair at one of the parishes in the Wichita Diocese years ago. A new pastor had just arrived, and he had decided to implement Stewardship within the parish. So, the parish went about running their first renewal, and they were surprised by the results. "The head of the Stewardship Committee there called me up and he says, 'I'm disappointed, because (parishioners) turned in their forms and only 50% of the people handed them in.'" Msgr.

McGread was surprised by the call, because in his experience a 50% response rate was wonderful. And he told the Committee chair so: "God bless you. You are very, very fortunate, that 50% turned them in," he said.

Indeed, it takes time for some people to experience a conversion of heart, to commit to live the Stewardship way of life. But it will happen. "Eventually they will turn in their cards," Msgr. McGread assures us, recalling his words of advice to that Stewardship committee chair. Don't be discouraged when you find that no one turned in a commitment card. Do not be discouraged when one year and another passes, and you haven't noticed the immense financial changes you had hoped to see. Stewardship is, indeed, discipleship lived out today, and, though it definitely takes time, your parishioners will learn by your example. They will respond to your invitation. They will give themselves to Jesus. It just takes time.

So, commit to live Stewardship. You will see a change in the hearts and lives of your people.

The 10 Most Important Ingredients
For A Successful Stewardship Way of Life:

So many pastors and lay leaders were asking the Steward-ship Committee at St. Francis of Assisi for advice and assistance in implementing the Stewardship way of life, that they put together a handout listing the 10 most important ingredients for a successful Stewardship way of life. According to the Stewardship Committee, these necessary ingredients are:

1. Belief – *The pastors and lay leaders must exhibit absolute trust and confidence in that way of life. They must really and truly believe it is God's way of living.*

2. Prayer – *We must be a prayerful people. Never begin a meeting without prayer. Jesus told us to "pray always," yet so often we say that we don't have time. We do have time. God gave us time. And we must make time for God of utmost importance. We can pray in short form and long form, with our own thinking and mental prayer as well as with physical expression. God has placed us on this earth, and He wants us to come to him. He offers us strength and support and love – much, much love. But He has given us free will and it is up to us to go to Him. He will not force us. We must realize that we are His children and that we cannot do anything without Him. We must constantly go to Him in prayer in order to deepen our relationship with Him. Only then, when we have a real relationship with God Himself, will we be able to live as Christian disciples, to build the Kingdom of God – drawing others to Jesus Christ.*

3. Spirituality – *Stewardship at its heart has nothing much to do with this life. The consequences of Stewardship are eternal. Whatever temporal manifestations of Steward-ship we achieve – a new rosary group in the parish,* *increased enrollment in adult education classes, even a priestly vocation from the parish – are worldly reminders that we all must be seeking a heavenly home.*

4. Have A Plan – Being that implementing the Steward- ship way of life is a long-term process, we need a plan. Without a properly thought out plan we will find ourselves going in circles trying to figure out where to start, and even once you've begun the life-long process of Steward- ship formation, education, and invitation, without a step- by-step plan, the goal often gets lost.

"One of the things that I find is that many parishes want to have a Stewardship way of life working in about 6-months to a year at the very most," Msgr. McGread remarks. "Whereas sometimes it takes two to three or as many as five years to get it really on a roll within the parish. It depends, in large part, on what your plan is and how educated your leaders and other parishioners are in regard to Stewardship."

5. Communication – The right hand must know what the left hand is doing. All of the parishioners must be made aware of what's going on within the parish. There must be constant open communication so that parishioners recognize that it is "their" parish, not "the pastor's." Also, we must provide the opportunity for people to volunteer. They also need to know, when they do volunteer, how long they are committing to serve (i.e. the head of the commit- tee serves for a year).

6. Hospitality – People need to feel welcomed to be part of the Stewardship way of life. As a parish, we need to truly love and care for one another and show one another that love, because our love for one another is, in part, an expression of the endless love God has for each one of us. Part of loving and welcoming everyone, which is so vital to the Stewardship way of life, is forgiveness. Sure, we are all bound to offend one another now and again. There are, undoubtedly, hurt feelings amidst the community, but we simply must love one another in spite of the offense or the hurt. Jesus tells us that. The parish is a place where everyone must feel comfortably at home, never alienated.

7. Consensus – Take a consensus at parish meetings as opposed to voting. It may take ten to fifteen minutes longer than voting does, but when people agree about what we are to do, no one goes home disappointed. No one feels outnumbered. In order to make a consensus, we need to keep talking until we come to that conclusion.

8. Inclusion – This means including everyone – the young people, middle-aged, old people, handicapped people – we're all part of God's people and we all need to be included to make this a successful process.

9. Gratitude – Sometimes we forget to say thank you. It is very important, first and foremost, to say thank you to God. We need to thank one another too - particularly the volunteers. Every gift of time, talent and treasure, no matter how small or insignificant, should call forth gratitude.

10. A Vision – Have a vision of what you want in your parish. We can look back at the early Church and the tremendous outpouring of Stewardship that they experienced as an early community. They shared everything with one another. They helped one another so that even the pagans could see how these Christians loved one another. Can we say that of our parish? Can we say that these people really love one another? Do they get to know one another, realizing that they're all God's children and working to build God's Kingdom here on Earth? Isn't that what we want for our parish? We must have a vision.

CHAPTER 5

THE BIRTH OF A NEW MINISTRY

When I first met Msgr. McGread at the International Catholic Stewardship Council (ICSC) Conference in 1997, I had no idea how our lives and ministries would intertwine just a few years later. I remember being impressed with this humble man who had contributed so much to the understanding of and practice of Stewardship as a disciple's way of life within the Catholic Church here in America.

At that time, I was running a management consulting firm. After over 25 plus years in public accounting, I was enjoying managing my own company and using my experience to help other companies with things like business plans, financial management, cost accounting services, etc.

Meanwhile, my eldest son, Eric McArdle, was running a marketing firm. His firm's focus was on developing marketing plans and marketing materials including surveys, newsletters and brochures for professional service organizations and non-profit companies.

It wasn't long before our firms would partner with Msgr. McGread's mission, and together we would work to encourage Stewardship at Catholic parishes and dioceses throughout the nation.

Our journey toward full-time Stewardship work began in 1996, before I personally met Msgr. McGread. Our parish pastor, Fr. Allan McDonald, was looking for a way to revitalize his parish (Church of the Most Holy Trinity, Augusta, Georgia – an inner-city parish of about 1,200 households) – both spiritually and materially. He had been preaching about Stewardship for close to four years at that point, and, on top of wanting his parishioners to embrace the Stewardship way of life, Fr. McDonald was eager to renovate the 150-year-old historic church building.

"It was literally beginning to fall apart," Fr. McDonald recalls. "The plaster was crumbling, the stained glass windows were leaking, the pipe organ was broken, and that's just a few of the issues that needed to be addressed."

It was going to take a great deal of time and a great deal of money, but Fr. McDonald knew it needed to get done. However, he did not want to do a traditional capital campaign in order to raise the funds. He felt like the "fund-raising" spirit of such a campaign would muddle the parishioners' understanding of true Stewardship, and he wanted Stewardship to be the parish's focus. What's more, he knew the necessary money could be obtained if the parishioners were practicing Stewardship.

He firmly believed that if the hearts of his people were converted and they began to involve themselves in the parish for the right reasons, the funds would come and they would see an increase to the regular weekly offertory as well.

"I was brought up in a household where the idea of tithing was a Protestant concept," Fr. McDonald remembers. "I can remember my father getting angry when the priests in our parish would speak about money. He would come home fuming. Usually the priest would preach about money when there was some crisis. And it wasn't done in as nice a manner in which Msgr. McGread preaches about Stewardship. It was more 'you need to do this,' and 'this is what we're lacking and if you were doing better we would be doing better.' So there was always a negative attitude about giving within my whole household."

Fr. McDonald's conversion of heart and his commitment to live the Stewardship way of life began in 1994, when two of his parishioners approached him about it. They had been invited into a life of Stewardship at their previous parish, and they believed that Holy Trinity needed to embrace Stewardship as a way of life. "They taught me, literally, about Catholic Stewardship as Msgr. McGread speaks about it," Fr. McDonald explains. "I have to tell you that I was extremely impressed by these lay people who had made a commitment to tithe as well as to give of their time and talent to the parish and to do so gratefully without grumbling or complaining. They saw this as a great opportunity for our parish in terms of renewal, in terms of discipleship, and in terms of spirituality. So they convinced me that I needed to go to a national convention on Stewardship, which I did."

When he attended his first ICSC Conference in 1994, Fr. McDonald was in awe. There were a large number of lay people in attendance, and the laity who were there seemed to be committed to Stewardship. For Father, it was still somewhat of a foreign concept, but he was learning that living Stewardship really did have the power to change hearts and minds and, in that, to greatly improve the life of the parish.

"I was really impressed with the laity who were into the spirituality of returning their gifts to God out of gratefulness for what God had given them, in terms of time, talent and treasure, and it just changed my whole attitude about tithing and all of the rest."

So, when Fr. McDonald returned home, he did so with renewed vigor, determined to live Stewardship both individually and together with his parish community.

"I finally made an intention to take a step toward tithing myself," Father remembers. "My first step was to tithe on my salary, then eventually it was my car allowance, and now I try to figure out what the value of my room and board is, the other perks that I get, what the total income package is, the gifts I would get in terms of stipends, etc., and I take my 10% pledge off the top. I can't ask anyone else to do it if I'm not doing it myself."

As he began to practice Stewardship personally, Fr. McDonald recognized some of the benefits of truly giving of his first fruits. He felt a change in his own heart, and he was ready to help his parishioners experience conversion of heart as well. Father was fired up! He was going to lead his people in the Stewardship way of life, and he was incredibly hopeful that it would change the dynamics of his parish for the better.

"During this time, we realized that we needed to get people more involved in the life of the parish, to get things going, to get volunteers participating in a variety of ways, and we needed to do something about our facilities that were falling apart around us," Fr. McDonald recalls. "I wanted to do it with Stewardship."

... And so began this new Stewardship ministry – thanks to the workings of the Holy Spirit!

"In the Spring of 1996, oddly enough, there was a parish meeting that Eric and his wife, Lisa, were attending," Fr. McDonald explains. "I mentioned to them that I wanted to do something about this church building and about Stewardship, and I wasn't exactly sure how we were going to go about doing it. At the same time, they were beginning a marketing firm that was not Stewardship related, but they worked with businesses providing a lot of P.R. and communication services. By the end of the meeting, they said, 'we'd like to talk to you, maybe we could help you with this process.' A few days later Eric came in with his dad, Don, who was our deacon, and I explained to them what I wanted to do, that I had bought into this focus on the spirituality of Stewardship. They said, 'we think we can help.' But what they wanted to do, believe it or not, was a traditional capital campaign. I told them 'no, that's not what I want to do,' and so I began to explain to them this concept of Stewardship, but they didn't really grasp it at first. I told them that they needed to go to a national Stewardship convention, which they did. And when they came back, they were converted."

Eric and Lisa attended their first ICSC conference in 1996. There, they first encountered Msgr. McGread. "I had heard a bit about him and the story of St. Francis from other people so I went to hear him talk at the conference," Eric says. "I wanted to learn more about what he did at St. Francis and how we could try and accomplish the same things at Holy Trinity."

The talk that Eric and Lisa heard was one Msgr. McGread had given many times before – sharing his personal experience and that of his parish in a very matter-of-fact way. "I remember being struck that he was a humble guy who talked the talk and had walked the walk," Eric says. "He was someone who knew what worked, what was right, and he wouldn't compromise."

Msgr. McGread's talk was one of many that Eric and Lisa heard during that conference, and the more they heard, the more they experienced a conversion, believing that Stewardship was, indeed, the way that they should live and the way in which they should help Fr. McDonald revitalize their home parish. "We were both struck by what people were saying in terms of what this Stewardship way of life is and how it can develop our personal faith walk and our relationship with Christ, while at the same time helping to develop our parish," Lisa recalls.

Upon returning to Augusta, Eric and Lisa shared their excitement and ideas with me and two others – my daughter, Shauna Occhipinti, who was working with me, and Sam Alzheimer who was working with Eric and Lisa at the time. It became obvious to all of us that we had a unique opportunity to use our two businesses to help serve a parish that we all loved. So both companies began to work together, and we formulated a plan that utilized our business and marketing services in a slightly different way, in a way that followed the outline that Msgr. McGread had laid out in his talk. "We put a process together that, at it's foundation, is very similar to what we still do today with parishes," remarks Eric. We like to call it the McGread approach in honor of all we learned from Msgr. McGread's own experiences. We presented Fr. McDonald with our Stewardship plan, which emphasized the spirituality of Stewardship and was focused on improving communication, education, and evangelization throughout the entire parish. And Fr. McDonald said, "Let's run with it."

So the work began. A spiritual retreat was held for the parish leaders. Monthly newsletters were created and mailed to all households in order to share the message of

Stewardship and invite parishioners to live the Stewardship way of life. Fr. McDonald preached consistently
about Stewardship from the pulpit. A parish survey was
conducted to ascertain parishioners' thoughts and
concerns about many areas of parish life. And a Stewardship Renewal was conducted during which everyone was
invited to make a commitment to share their time, talent
and treasure with the parish. Included with the Stewardship Renewal process was information about the renovations needed for the church building and parishioners
were asked to make a separate financial pledge for this
need, which would go above and beyond their commitment to the weekly offertory.

The Stewardship initiative at Holy Trinity was pick-
ing up, and the people were responding. It seemed that,
with a little help from our professional abilities, Fr.
McDonald was able to follow the example of Msgr.
McGread and implement the Stewardship way of life in
his parish, which, as a result of Father's efforts, was
improving drastically in a very short period of time.

After a year of this increased focus on Stewardship,
Most Holy Trinity saw amazing results. Mass attendance
had increased, and the parish ministries were coming
back to life as more parishioners became involved in
both existing and in new ministries. "That first year, we
started about fifteen new parish ministries, and they
filled up with people," Eric remembers. In addition, the
parish offertory saw an increase of over $100,000 that

first year. At the same time, the parish raised $1.5 million for the restoration project.

Not only had Fr. McDonald's dream been possible, but he watched it come true. And with it, he watched his parish flourish with a renewed understanding of Stewardship.

"We were able to meet the needs of the parish not only in terms of our fiscal needs, but also the spiritual and ministerial needs, getting more people involved in the life of our parish and our various ministries," recalls Fr. McDonald. "We have a soup kitchen downtown, which is very ecumenical, and a significant number of our own parishioners began volunteering for that. Our involvement in Catholic Social Services increased. We were able to help with Habitat for Humanity and began a sister parish relationship with a parish in Tbilisi, Georgia (formerly part of the Soviet Union)." This relationship is one that Fr. McDonald speaks about with great pride, because it is a parishioner-initiated program that has allowed the parish to reach far beyond itself, and even its own community, in order to serve their Catholic brothers and sisters in need.

"One of my parishioners wanted to begin this outreach that he called, *Georgia to Georgia with Love*," Fr. McDonald says. "The religious component was that we, at Most Holy Trinity, would form a sister relationship with the one Catholic parish that remained open during communism in the Soviet Union in Tblisi, Georgia - Sts.

Peter and Paul. Over the years since we've had this sister parish relationship, we've been able to tithe to them a certain portion of our income." And, in addition to simply helping those in need, Father says, the sister parish relationship has helped the people at Most Holy Trinity as well. "It brought about a stronger awareness within our parish about our interconnectedness to the Catholics in the former Soviet Union who were coming out from under the claws of communism. This, in turn, brought about a deeper awareness of our interconnectedness with the Church throughout the world."

Other developments included a growing number of parishioners making commitments to pray daily at one of the two adoration chapels in the area. "We had more catechists coming forward for CCD. Our RCIA program became very active, with a number of parishioners involved as sponsors, catechists, hospitality, etc. We saw an increase in liturgical ministries and in participation with our choir."

The financial results of this increased focus on Stewardship impacted Most Holy Trinity in ways Fr. McDonald had hoped it would. In conjunction with the increased involvement of parishioners in the life of the parish through the gifts of their time and talent – and the increase in the weekly offertory, the financial commitments from parishioners made it possible to fully restore the church building. "We renovated the entire interior," says Fr. McDonald. "We moved the altar, re-did the three stained glass windows above the altar, which were as old as the church, expanded the choir loft, added a new sacristy, put a new roof on, new sound system, new pulpit, new chairs, and a few other odds and ends. All of that came to about $1.5 million and not once did we have to borrow money. It was like a miracle," he says. "It was like the multiplication of the loaves and fishes. My bookkeeper would keep saying to me, 'We're getting to the point we need to pay this bill, I think we're going to have to borrow money.' But we never had to."

Holy Trinity was changing. They were becoming a new parish family. They were recognizing the gracious generosity and the goodness of the Lord and were willing and even eager to return their first fruits to the Lord in gratitude. The parishioners' relationships with one another were deepening, and, most importantly, their faith lives were fueled to new heights. It was incredible for Fr. McDonald to witness, but it was even more powerful for him to experience these changes alongside his parishioners. Together, they were becoming a Stewardship people, twentieth century disciples. It was undeniable.

Holy Trinity's Stewardship efforts were recognized by the International Catholic Stewardship Conference (ICSC) at their 1997 conference when they presented Most Holy Trinity with the "Total Parish Stewardship Award". They received the award again in 1998.

At this point, we began to hear from other parishes that were interested in similar services. So we officially merged our two companies into one and began formulating a plan for marketing our newly organized services to other Catholic parishes. The newly developed company slowly grew, mainly by word of mouth.

During this time, we continued our management consulting and marketing work, but it was becoming quite clear that this new Stewardship ministry was our calling.

Then in late 1999, after much prayer and discussion, the decision was made to begin focusing all of our energy and resources on serving Catholic parishes exclusively under the name of Catholic Stewardship Consultants. This was not an easy decision, and it wasn't one based on sophisticated business modeling or financial forecasting. However, everyone involved in the company felt God was calling us in this direction. We decided to take a leap of faith and trust that God would guide us.

Now, many years later, we at Catholic Stewardship Consultants have been blessed to serve over 140 parishes throughout the country, and we are honored to continue serving everyone we can.

We are definitely proud of what we've been able to do. Yet, we see our work more as a ministry than a business. We are trying to help pastors help their parishioners become better disciples. We try to ground everything we do in the spirituality of Stewardship. We know beyond a shadow of a doubt that God has helped us to become the organization we are today, and we pray that He will continue to lead us toward His will in the future.

I believe that all we have been able to help parishes achieve is due to the work of the Lord Himself and the priceless guidance of Msgr. McGread. Early on we began to run ideas about our process by Msgr. McGread. We knew he wouldn't hesitate to tell us if we were losing focus or if we were getting sidetracked in our spiritual approach to Stewardship. After a few years of serving as an informal advisor, Msgr. McGread graciously agreed to serve as our primary advisor.

"I have been asked to work with many companies over the years, but Catholic Stewardship Consultants is the only one I have found that truly understands the spirituality of Stewardship," remarks Msgr. McGread. "In my work with Deacon Don, Eric, and the staff, I have been deeply impressed with their commitment to the Church. We share the same vision of Stewardship – not as a campaign or program, but as a way of life. In their work with parishes, Catholic Stewardship Consultants uses the same approach I used at St. Francis. They begin by working with the leaders and emphasizing spirituality. They help improve communication, education, and evangelization throughout the entire parish."

The more we at Catholic Stewardship Consultants work with Msgr. McGread, the more we recognize what a tremendous gift he is to the Church, especially in the area of Stewardship. We want to help others learn from him.

In order to try and accomplish this, we decided to host a Stewardship conference in his backyard and bring pastors and lay leaders to him. In 2003, we worked closely with him to host the first-ever Msgr. McGread Stewardship Conference near his home in Wichita, Kansas. We have since held at least two of these conferences each year, which has allowed hundreds of parishes across the country to learn from Msgr. McGread first-hand. We've also added regional and diocesan conferences from time to time when requested. At each conference we bring together pastors and parish leaders to train them in the spirituality and practice of Stewardship, as envisioned by Msgr. McGread. These pastors and parish leaders then take this message back home and help plant the seeds of Stewardship within the hearts and lives of their own parishioners.

PART II

STEWARDSHIP LIVED THROUGHOUT THE COUNTRY

CHAPTER 6

A PARISH CONVERTED

St. John the Apostle Catholic Church – Minot, ND

Fr. David Zimmer
Diocese of Bismarck
Pastor of St. John the Apostle Catholic Church Minot, ND
Living Stewardship six years

It may seem strange for a parish priest who was born and raised a Catholic to call himself a convert, but that is exactly how Fr. Dave Zimmer — pastor of St. John the Apostle Catholic Church in Minot, N.D. — sees himself.

"I *am* a convert," he says with sincere conviction in his voice. "I am a convert to the Stewardship way of life."

As he tells his story, Fr. Dave radiates with pure joy and excitement. He was convicted by the Holy Spirit and now he is fueled by the fire of the Spirit to spread the message.

As Fr. Dave tells it, his story begins about six years ago when he sat in a small conference room in Wichita, Kansas, and listened to renowned Stewardship pioneer Msgr. Thomas McGread tell the story of St. Francis of Assisi parish. But as Fr. Dave continues to reflect on his "conversion" to the Stewardship way of life, he also reminisces of times when the Spirit was prodding him. Surely, God had been working in his life, bringing him to a place where he would be ready to accept the message of Stewardship when Msgr. McGread spoke directly to his heart.

Some years earlier, Fr. Dave was working in the Diocese of Bismarck Pastoral Center. His office sat next to that of the diocesan development director, Ron Schatz. Ron believed Stewardship should be lived as a way of life by all Catholics. So, he was constantly trying to convince others of the importance of Stewardship. Fr. Dave was not exempt from Ron's efforts.

"He would come out of his office and start talking to me about Stewardship," Fr. Dave remembers, "and I would tell him, 'don't talk to me about it.'"

As far as Fr. Dave was concerned, the word Stewardship was synonymous with fundraising, and he wanted nothing to do with Ron's "fundraising" efforts. But Ron did not give up. "'It's not about fundraising,' he would continue," Fr. Dave recalls. "But I would just walk away."

He walked away, that is, until God spoke so loudly through Ron's efforts that Fr. Dave couldn't help but hear.

In January 2005, Ron sent Father a brochure for the Msgr. McGread Conference in Wichita. That was the last straw. Fr. Dave finally gave in! He attended the conference and it was there that his personal conversion of heart took place.

"I was in the fourth row back, in the fourth chair," Fr Dave says, remembering the Holy Spirit speaking to him quite clearly.

"I knew Ron was right," he explains. "Stewardship is not about fundraising, and I had to humbly admit that, up until then, I knew nothing about what it means to live Stewardship."

Yet, as Father sat and listened to talk after talk during that conference, he began to understand. Stewardship is about discipleship. It is about evangelization. Living Stewardship means living our Faith on a daily basis, here and now.

He had recently become pastor at St. John, a small parish of about 655 families in the small town of Minot, N.D., and he was excited to bring the message of Stewardship back to his people.

When Fr. Dave arrived back in Minot, still the new pastor – he'd only been there for a year – on the heels of the previous pastor's 32-year stint, Fr. Dave began to communicate the message of Stewardship to the parish leaders.

"I called an emergency parish council meeting and began telling the members all about what I had heard in

Wichita," Fr. Dave remembers. "I was ecstatic. I mean, they had never seen me so excited about anything. And their reaction to my enthusiasm was, 'that's nice.'"

Needless to say, the leaders were not really on board with Father, who believed the Stewardship way of life was what their parish needed.

"They just didn't get it," Fr. Dave recalls.

But he was not deterred. In fact, Father was so convinced that Stewardship was the way of life that all Catholics should live that he was determined to convince his leaders.

It turns out that convincing them didn't actually take too long. The following August, Fr. Dave returned to Wichita, this time with a few of his parish leaders in tow. Together they listened to the experience of many pastors and lay leaders, and that's all it took! They were convinced! They wanted to live as Christ's disciples today. They wanted to live Stewardship, and they wanted to bring the message back to the people of their parish.

And so they did.

"We unanimously decided to become a Stewardship parish," Fr. Dave explains. They immediately set out in an effort to do that.

Putting their desire into action, it would turn out, would not be easy for St. John. A small parish with very little staff and no room to hire more, the people of St. John needed help.

"We wanted to begin this new chapter in our life," Fr. Dave says, "but we needed help to write the chapter." After all, Father was aware, having heard the stories of so many others during his time in Wichita, that implementing the Stewardship way of life takes a lot of effort.

"That's where our 'satellite office' in Augusta, Georgia comes in," Father explains with great joy. "We hired Catholic Stewardship Consultants, and immediately, together with them, we began to implement Stewardship at our parish."

They began with meeting after meeting, gathering the parish leaders together to ensure that everyone was on the same page, and that everyone understood what the Stewardship way of life would mean for St. John. Although, Father admits, "I don't think everyone really knew what they were signing up for at the time." Yet, they all were on board, and, it seems, God took over from there.

With the help of Catholic Stewardship Consultants, St. John had a parish retreat, emphasizing the spiritual foundation of the Stewardship way of life, and they began to publish a monthly newsletter, which served to evangelize, educate, and inform all of the St. John parishioners – active and non-active.

Things were taking off for them. In fact, Fr. Dave admits, "I don't think we realized how fertile our soil was. Our parish soil was ready for the Stewardship seed to be planted. We just needed to make ourselves aware of it."

There was so much going on at St. John, and they didn't realize it. So many parishioners were already giving of themselves. And by implementing Stewardship as a way of life for his parishioners, Fr. Dave was able to emphasize this, calling everyone to give more of themselves.

That fall, St. John held their first Stewardship Renewal, and the results were amazing. "The fire was starting to spread," Fr. Dave says. "Stewardship was starting to take on a life of its own, and I could see it changing people."

What Father noticed was only reinforced by the results of their first renewal. They had a 35% response rate — a rate much greater than the national average. They had 731 parishioners who made personal commitments of time, 758 parishioners who committed to participate in parish ministries, and the offertory went up 40%. Fr. Dave was amazed. Stewardship was taking root, and the parish of St. John "would never be the same," Father says.

Yet, as far as Fr. Dave is concerned, those statistics are not the indicators of success at St. John. "I cannot look at statistics to measure the success of the Stewardship way of life," he says. Rather, he looks at the daily lives of his people, and Father is sure that the parish of St. John is definitely living as present-day disciples of Christ.

"We have become more prayerful, joyful, and hopeful people. You can see it in the faces and the lives of the people. You can feel it in their presence." St. John is a different place today than it was six years ago. They continue to commit themselves, daily, to Christ.

The Holy Spirit has not ceased His work in Minot! Just as He began a stirring in the heart of Fr. Dave years ago, he continues to stir up the fire in the hearts of the whole parish. In truth, they are all converts, thanks be to God!

CHAPTER 7

A DECISION WITH DESTINY

St. Mary on the Hill Catholic Church – Augusta, GA

Msgr. Jim Costigan
Diocese of Savannah
Pastor of St. Mary on the Hill Catholic Church Augusta, GA
for 28 years
Current Pastor of St. Peter the Apostle Catholic Church
Savannah, GA
Living Stewardship for 24 years

Growing up in Ireland, the Costigan family of seven lived only a half mile from St. Bridget Church in Clonakenny, Ireland where Msgr. Jim Costigan's dad gave of his time doing repairs and upkeep. While there was no such term for Stewardship back then, Msgr. Costigan recognized his father's actions, years later, as giving of his time and talent. Then came the day when his dad's treasure would also be counted on. It was a moment that impacted young Jim Costigan deeply.

"Something significant happened one morning at the breakfast table that stuck with me," he says. "I was ten years of age, with two brothers and two sisters. My mother turned to my dad during breakfast and said, 'You know dad, there's a collection today at our parish.' They didn't have a regular collection every Sunday back in those days. Instead, the parish held collections when there was a specific need – church upkeep, care for the priests, etc. So my father took out his wallet and he put down two pounds, probably the equivalent at that time of about $6.00, which was quite a lot of money. We weren't by any means large farmers and we were not well off, but my father felt that was what he needed to give. And mother looked at him and said, 'You know they're putting a new roof on the church.' There was a long pause of silence. Then after a moment he said, 'You know the lads are going back to school and they need new boots and clothes.' I could hear the pain in his voice as he thought about all of the expenses. Then my father opened his wallet and he put down two more pounds. He was going to give the church the equivalent of $12.00."

Though Msgr. Costigan's father knew that he and his family had little money, he recognized his need to give back to God for the gifts he and his family had been given, and he chose to put God first.

Msgr. Costigan has never forgotten the example of his father giving to the church out of his "first-fruits". "When I went to the seminary, although I had never heard about Stewardship, I knew that one day I'd be asking people, like my father, to help me put a roof on a church or something of the sort. And I knew that they'd be taking their wallets out and they'd be calculating how much this was going to cost them."

Two and a half years after being ordained, Msgr. Costigan found himself in the role of Pastoral Administrator at Sacred Heart Church in Augusta, Georgia. "It was an old church that needed work, and I had to stand before the congregation and ask for money," Msgr. Costigan says. "It wasn't easy. I remembered the day my father took four pounds out of his wallet, and it pained me to ask for the money." It likely also pained parishioners, who, as Msgr. Costigan recalled, were simply instructed to give until it hurt. "You see, when people were reaching for their wallets, they found that it hurt rather quickly," Msgr. Costigan quips. "And that's what they knew of giving their treasure." The thing that Msgr. Costigan found strange about the old standard of giving was that there was no real measure. "I knew there had to be a better way." With the kind of system that simply instructs you to give until it hurts, there is no guide for either the asker or giver - no base to operate from. "When does one know when they are doing the right thing?" asks Msgr. Costigan. "Even the precept of the

Church didn't give any guidance except to say that people were to give to the support of their pastors."

Msgr. Costigan always felt that there had to be a better way to encourage parishioners to support the Church in the way God calls us to. "The better way of course is Stewardship," Msgr. Costigan now knows. "It's the way we empower people to live their faith. It's the way people know what's right, and it helps us to not feel guilty about enjoying the normal pleasures of life. Stewardship is a complete lifestyle, a life of total accountability and responsibility acknowledging God as Creator and Owner of all. As disciples of Christ, stewards see themselves as caretakers of all God's gifts. Gratitude for these gifts is expressed in prayer and worship and by eagerly sharing these gifts – time, talent, and treasure – out of love of God and one another."

While it is the financial giving aspect that likely first comes to mind when parishioners hear the word *Stewardship*, Msgr. Costigan is quick to point out that Stewardship consists of three different, but equally important, precepts to which all Christians are called. "When I think about Stewardship," Msgr. Costigan says, "it's not just about money. Time and talent are so significant and so important."

Msgr. Costigan believes that the message of the old *Baltimore Catechism* is still alive and well in today's message of Stewardship. "Why did God make us?" Msgr. Costigan asks. Then, answering his own question, he

explains, "In the *Baltimore Catechism* we have a Stewardship definition – to know, to love and to serve Him - head,
heart, and hands. Whichever way you look at that definition, through Stewardship you are simply inviting people
to be part of the Catholic Church – to live the Faith, to
know, love, and serve the Lord."

In fact, Msgr. Costigan believes, much like Msgr.
McGread does, that invitation is where Stewardship
starts. He believes that when we invite people to get
involved, we sow the seeds of Stewardship. "You ask
parishioners to be involved, to do something, maybe it's
only taking the basket up or whatever it is, and the next
thing you know they show up and become involved," he
explains, noting what he has seen happen time and again
for his own parishioners. "They are drawn in through
that service. They are touched in their hearts."

Msgr. Costigan's Own Conversion to the Stewardship Way of Life

Msgr. Costigan didn't always fully understand the
Stewardship way of life. He had to experience his own
conversion of heart before he could lead his parishioners
to embrace Stewardship as a way of life. His conversion
was a long journey that took place, in large part, at the
parish he pastored for 28 years – St. Mary on the Hill in
Augusta, Georgia.

"I came into Stewardship by the back door in a
sense," Msgr. Costigan recalls. "I arrived at St. Mary on

the Hill in 1982. At the time, St. Mary's had 1,300 families and a weekly offertory of $8,000. It is a suburban upper middle-class parish. But you would never know it to look at the budget. We had a school with just over 500 children and all of our buildings were in need of upgrading."

Meanwhile, his friend, Fr. Kevin Boland (the now-Bishop Boland of the Diocese of Savannah), was the pastor of St. Anne in Columbus, Georgia. "He wanted to improve their school," recalls Msgr. Costigan. "So, together, we decided to hire a development director. She would spend half time at each parish, and help us develop the schools. I recall Fr. Boland suggesting we go to a workshop to learn something about how to use a development director, about how to oversee this new person."

So Msgr. Costigan and Fr. Boland went to a development conference in Arizona in 1985. During the conference, they heard Msgr. McGread speak for the first time.

At the time, Msgr. Costigan was working to implement the concept of sacrificial giving in the life of his parish. The concept was "give until it hurts," and Msgr. Costigan wanted his parishioners to give to the Lord.

But he found that parishioners were not very receptive to the idea of sacrificial giving. "I found that most people started to hurt quickly even before they opened their wallets," Msgr. Costigan recalls. Although he did find that his preaching about sacrificial giving began to open up the minds of his parishioners to give in a sacrificial way, he was never completely satisfied with the concept.

When he heard Msgr. McGread speak at that conference in 1985, Msgr. McGread's words struck him to the core. "He spoke about giving in a different way," Msgr. Costigan remembers. "It clicked with me that, at a minimum, Stewardship was a much better way of addressing giving."

The following year, Msgr. Costigan and Fr. Boland went to an International Catholic Stewardship Conference in Boston. There, they met Msgr. McGread personally. He was the keynote speaker for the conference. So, once again, they heard him talk. Then they spoke with him.

At that time, St. Francis had a weekly offertory of $60,000, no tuition for their parish school, perpetual adoration, and hundreds of parishioners gave of their Time and Talent. "We said the only way we can believe this is to see it," Msgr. Costigan remarks. So when Msgr. McGread invited the two priests to visit St. Francis, they quickly accepted. And the rest, as they say, is history. "We came home and put together three Sundays of Stewardship talks – with a priest, parish couples and singles. I addressed Stewardship regularly in my homilies, and we worked toward looking at giving of ourselves through Stewardship. I encouraged the parishioners to give of themselves out of gratitude to God for all He has given them. And I saw a difference in them! The offertory went up a whopping 37% that first year. It was a new life for all of us. It was like a heart transplant."

The dramatic increases in St. Mary on the Hill's offer-tory, after Msgr. Costigan introduced Stewardship as a way of life to the parish in 1986, allowed the parish to move forward with much-needed upgrades to the parish facilities. "In the ensuing years, we spent about $6 million on our parish buildings and renovated our school for $5 million. The parish did conduct one capital campaign in the following years. Through it, they raised $2 million, but the rest of the funds were raised through the parish-ioners' embrace of Stewardship as a way of life.

"Then in 1995, we felt we had reached a plateau and weren't going anywhere," Msgr. Costigan remembers. "I wanted the Stewardship way of life to continue having a deep impact on the life of the parish. I didn't want people to become complacent. So, I discussed things with our parish leaders, and together we wondered if we could make all our parish ministries, including our parish school, Stewardship based. Could we become a total Stewardship parish like St. Francis was? With that in mind, we brought in the big guns for our annual renewal-Msgr. Thomas McGread. His message to our people was very simple, 'you've got to make a leap of faith.'" But Msgr. Costigan would soon find that taking this leap of faith wouldn't be so easy for him.

The first time the Finance Commission met after Msgr. McGread's visit, they discussed the possibility of supporting the parish school through Stewardship. "Essentially we were talking of tagging on $1.5 million to the church budget for the school and PRE (Parish Religious Education). We agreed to conduct some key group meetings with people involved with the school, PRE, and parish life," Msgr. Costigan recalls. "Then we did a survey. The Finance Commission called a meeting to look at the survey results and it was obvious by the results that we were not ready to do this yet. When I got home that evening there was a message from the chairperson asking me to meet with her over lunch. On behalf of the parish, she asked me to lead them in this leap of faith, or at least to let them try. ***Think about this for a moment. The people in the pews are asking me, the man at the pulpit and altar, the man of faith himself, to take a leap of faith.*** Of course she knew I was shaking at the knees. I wasn't prepared to make a "leap of faith". I can hardly describe the agony of the next three days. I didn't sleep, eat or handle work. At an earlier time in my life, I almost left the priesthood over a church being closed and there were many other bumps along the way of my faith life. But you talk about crises - this measured up there with those."

But then, three days later, Msgr. Costigan received confirmation from the Lord about what he was to do. "The Lord let me have it with a 2-by-4 over the head," he says. "I was struggling with living as a man of faith versus the idea of seeing a sign on the front lawn declaring the church bankrupt. On the third night, at about 3:00 a.m. as I was pacing around my room, I thought to myself, 'When all else fails, look in the Bible.' A decision was due to the Finance Committee in the morning, so I knew I had to say yes or no to completely living Stewardship as a parish. As I opened my Bible there it was, 'put your trust in the Lord,' jumping out at me."

Msgr. Costigan's eyes read over these verses from Malachi.

"For I, the Lord, do not change; therefore you, O sons of Jacob, are not consumed. From the days of your fathers you have turned aside from my statutes and have not kept them. Return to me, and I will return to you, says the LORD of hosts. But you say, 'How shall we return?' Will man rob God? Yet you are robbing me. But you say, 'How are we robbing thee?' In your tithes and offerings. You are cursed with a curse, for you are robbing me; the whole nation of you. Bring the full tithes into the storehouse, that there may be food in my house; and thereby put me to the test, says the Lord of hosts, if I will not open the window of heaven for you and pour down for you an overflowing blessing. I will rebuke the devourer for you, so that it will not destroy the fruits of your soil; and your vine in the field shall not fail to bear, says the Lord of hosts. Then all nations will call you blessed, for you will be the land of delight, says the Lord of hosts."

(Malachi 3:6-12)

This scripture passage was all Msgr. Costigan needed. He knew, right then, what his answer would be that next morning. He was now ready to lead his parish in taking a leap of faith. And beginning with the 1996-1997 school year, St. Mary on the Hill School became fully funded by the parishioners' Stewardship way of life.

"We asked all parishioners to contribute 8% to the parish, 1% to the diocese and 1% to other charities. But it wasn't just the financial giving that was encouraged. I asked them to give of their whole selves in gratitude to the Lord for His many gifts." They were asked to give of their time, talents, and treasure.

What Msgr. Costigan found hard to believe could happen, when he first heard Msgr. McGread's story about St. Francis, he was now watching happen in his own parish. When Msgr. Costigan was transferred from St. Mary's in 2002, St. Mary's weekly offertory was averaging over $60,000 a week. "In addition, we were giving to the diocesan campaign every year - our goal was $130,000 and we usually went a third or so over that each year. One year, the diocese did a campaign for renovations of the Cathedral. Our goal was to raise $1.1 million, and yet we were able to offer the diocese $1.5. We tithed 10% of our offertory to charity. We completed a $5 million building project on the school without conducting a capital campaign. All of our parish ministries and outreach efforts were funded through the weekly offertory. We have a no-tuition school. We started a Senior Center. St. Mary's now has perpetual adoration. Mass attendance continues to increase and the level of parishioner involvement in parish ministries continues to increase."

Msgr. Costigan knows firsthand that Stewardship works. It is the proper response of Christian disciples, and, through Stewardship, we all grow closer to Christ and His Church, and we are all strengthened in faith as a result. Through Stewardship our parishes are changed.

"Now, I'm not going to say it's easy," Msgr. Costigan says. "It's not. But it is a holistic approach. Stewardship is about changing hearts, not heads. And that's the big difference between a Stewardship way of life and fund drive orientation. Capital campaigns are driven by parish financial needs and we drive our people to achieve the goals we desire based on the funds we need. To achieve this we bring in fund drive people - we get the amount in and off we go - it is a drive. Stewardship is totally different. We, the pastors, are the leaders - the shepherd. A shepherd is out front calling his sheep while a herdsman is behind driving his sheep. Both may get to the destination, but it's a very different approach."

Msgr. Costigan does not believe in asking people to do what he himself is not prepared to do. He has committed to living a Stewardship way of life. "Every Sunday I place my envelope in the basket together with the gifts of the parishioners. I feel good about what I do. I don't need to make any apologies to anybody for my lifestyle. I play golf, have a boat, etc. That's what I like about this too for the people. If we do what is expected, and we know what God expects, then we can enjoy life as it were."

Now, Stewardship takes time, Msgr. Costigan cautions. "We have to be patient and let God change the hearts, and when it happens it's for a lifetime. People who practice Stewardship learn first-hand that God will not be outdone in generosity. Of course the television evangelists would have us believe that if we give to God, God will see to it that the giver will receive a great windfall. But this is a false message. Good stewards do not give to get, they are giving out of gratitude. One veteran put it this way 'Ever since I accepted Christ's Stewardship mandate, I've become increasingly sensitized to the many gifts and blessings God has bestowed on me and my family every day – so many things I used to take for granted. I can't begin to thank God enough.' Yes, Stewardship involves a leap of faith. But if we're willing to take that leap, the blessings we will receive are immeasurable both for us as individuals and for our parishes."

What Fr. Costigan Sees As Important In Developing Stewardship as A way Of life In Your Parish

<u>The Pastor's Role in Stewardship:</u> If the pastor doesn't preach, teach and live it, the parish won't either. In their pastoral letter, *Stewardship, a Disciple's Response*, the US Bishops express it very clearly. "We are ALL

stewards of the church." The adage "we have a greater need to give than the Church does to receive" is surely true of the pastor. If true discipleship has Stewardship as its response, then we pastors, more than anyone else, must live the life of good stewards. If we "talk the talk" then we must "walk the walk".

<u>Stewardship = Changing Hearts - It Lasts Forever:</u> Stewardship enriches the lives of the people, and they take responsibility for the mission of Christ. They become disciples in a fuller sense. "Give a man a loaf of bread and you feed him for a day - give him a pound of seed and you feed him for life." You take people from the idea of "I *go* to church at St. Mary's Parish, to "I *belong* to St. Mary's Parish."

<u>Changing Attitudes:</u> Time, talent, and treasure are the only things we have to share and we have them only briefly.

A great area of parish life to begin instilling this change of attitude is Baptismal Preparation. Here the pastor has an opportunity to bring about a renewal of the couple's commitment to Christian discipleship. In addition, during Confirmation Preparation, you can involve both the parents and the child/youth in service projects. Use these times of sacramental preparation to invite parishioners to embrace the Stewardship way of life.

<u>Education:</u> Education is a key element to a successful Stewardship process. It needs to be ongoing, constant, year-round. Some educational tools include:

- <u>Weekly Bulletin</u> – Include notes from the pastor. I know pastors who have never written a note for their bulletins. That is a missed opportunity. The first thing people should see when they open the bulletin is the pastor's comments, and they should be meant to educate, inform, and evangelize your parishioners. Bulletin enclosures are also great educational resources. For a few cents a copy once a month, these inserts can put some Stewardship ideals & ideas before your parishioners.

- <u>Monthly Newsletter</u> – The newsletter is more detailed than the weekly bulletin. It provides more information about parish ministries and about parishioners who are living as good stewards. Through newsletter articles, parishioners are drawn into the life of the parish in a deeper way.

- <u>Teaching opportunities</u>: Look for opportunities to educate parishioners in a variety of settings – both with the parish at large and with smaller groups. These smaller groups can include the school and religious education parents, parish committees, staff, etc. Here the pastor can do a more in-depth study/reflection on the scriptural and theological basis for Stewardship than he can give during his weekly homily. These gatherings may be tedious, but they are well worth the effort.

<u>Stewardship Committee:</u> Pick the right people to serve on your Stewardship Committee and they will be worth their weight in gold.

<u>Live by Example:</u> Examine your own lifestyle as to the kind of Stewardship life you live. Live by example. We priests preach, but sometimes we don't think our words apply first to ourselves. I can tell you putting an envelope in the basket each week is the most powerful sermon. Showing up on the Habitat for Humanity site with a hammer is powerful. Not everybody is into that, but one must be into something. I don't believe in asking anybody to do anything I don't do myself.

<u>Preach about Stewardship:</u> Make it a priority for the pastor to preach during the annual Stewardship Renewal and incorporate the Stewardship message into homilies whenever possible.

<u>Prayer:</u> Encourage people to pray for the parish – think of others rather than self. Some parishes even write Stewardship prayers. Below is St. Mary's Stewardship Prayer:

Loving God, we come to you in thanksgiving, knowing all that we are and all that we have is a gift from you. Speak your words into the depths of our

> *souls, that we may hear you clearly. Give us the*
> *wisdom and insight to understand your will for us,*
> *and the fervor to fulfill our good intentions. We*
> *offer our gifts of time, talent, and treasure to you*
> *as a true act of faith, to reflect our love for you and*
> *our neighbor. Help us to reach out to others as you,*
> *our God, have reached out to us.*

<u>Tithing:</u> Be a tithing parish. This is very important.

<u>Annual Stewardship Renewal:</u> Parishioners need to make annual commitments of time, talent and treasure.

<u>Be Faithful:</u> Focus on being faithful, not necessarily on short-term financial success. This is where living a Stewardship way of life is vastly different than the "fundraising" mentality.

<u>Be Thankful:</u> Express thanks to people through your pastor's letters, appreciation gatherings, and from the pulpit.

Why Priests Are Unhappy Talking About Money

Msgr. Costigan has found that there are a number of reasons why priests are unhappy talking about money with their people, and the people, likewise, are unhappy hearing about money.

1. The first reason, he believes, is a misconception about an often-used passage in scripture from 1 Timothy:

    Teach and urge these duties. But those who want to be rich fall into temptation and are trapped by many senseless and harmful desires that plunge people into ruin and destruction. For the love of money is a root of all kinds of evil, and in their eagerness to be rich some have wandered away from the faith and pierced themselves with many pains. (1 Tim. 6:2-10)

    In this passage we learn that "the love of money is a root of all kinds of evil" not that "money is the root of all evil". While money is used for evil purposes it is not evil in itself. Money is necessary for corporal and spiritual works of mercy.

2. A second source of reluctance to address money with our parishioners can arise from a priest's own lack of theological education and spiritual formation regarding the use of money and developing a spirituality of discipleship that ties in treasure.

3. Also, Msgr. Costigan believes that priests have difficulty speaking of money because of the lifestyle they themselves enjoy. Some priests live in comfortable rectories, drive new cars every two

to three years, plan trips to Europe or the Caribbean for a winter break, and enjoy eating in the best restaurants. Many pastors have full health and retirement plans. Meanwhile, many parishioners are struggling with mortgages, tuition, car payments, food, and insurance. They are working hard feeding, clothing and educating their children while also saving for their own retirement. So, the pastor is often hesitant to ask them to put more money in the collection basket.

4. Another reason why money is often an uncomfortable subject is that most Catholics still operate on the immigrant church's idea that we "give to a need". One pastor called this (PTB) pay the bills. PTB parishioners give from a sense of duty or obligation. The amount they give is often determined by how the person feels that particular day or at the moment. Their gifts are based on an attitude "tell me how much you need Father, and I'll decide how much I want to give." The PTB are, no mistake about it, quite generous, but only after they are convinced of the need. They rarely give out of a sense of gratitude or the joy of giving to the ministry of Christ and His Church. They don't make the connection, because pastors have not made the connection for them. The biblical concept of tithing is not a consideration.

The number one reason people give to any institution is belief in what it does and its purposes. This raises some questions, then, for us. If the fundamental reason we exist is by reason of belief, then why doesn't this translate into our giving? The Church is different from any other institution because it has a divine mandate. It is the way the Father has ordained His business to be done. The Church is doing the work of Christ. We are talking about discipleship here.

We live in a culture that deifies accumulation of wealth. Practicing Stewardship in the United States is counter-cultural. But more and more Catholics are looking for a way to answer God's call and live life in a more holistic way. Many are choosing to embrace a Stewardship way of life. Whatever we do to educate our parishioners about Stewardship can only help to enrich their lives.

A View from the Pew:
A Big Leap of Faith, an Even Bigger Pay Off

When Pia Hagler thinks back to her life at St. Mary's in the late 1980's, when Msgr. Costigan first began challenging his parishioners to embrace Stewardship as a way of life, she recalls most vividly the necessary leap of faith. She is quick to thank God for giving her the courage to take that leap, a leap that has impacted all areas of her life for the better!

Pia and her husband, Mike, had been parishioners together since 1980. Mike grew up as a member of St. Mary's, and Pia joined the parish after she and Mike married and moved back to the area. It was indeed their parish home. They were involved by serving the parish when they saw a need. But then something changed that would deepen their involvement. Pia remembers listening to Msgr. Costigan's homilies about giving of our first fruits, and suddenly "a light went off," she says.

"He started talking about our need to give, and his homilies really heightened my awareness. I thought we were doing well. We were giving something financially and we were involved to some degree, but as Monsignor talked about how easy it is for us to indulge in things like cable TV and going out to eat and then giving what we can 'afford' rather than giving of our first fruits – in time, talent, and treasure – I realized that we really weren't doing all that we could or, for that matter, what we should."

With that, the Haglers began increasing their involvement in the life of the parish. Pia participated in the Parish Council of Catholic Women and the Parish Life Committee. Mike, meanwhile, became a member of the Finance Committee, the Parish Council, the Handy Dads ministry, and he made himself available whenever Msgr. Costigan needed something.

"He has financial expertise," Pia explains. "So Monsignor would call on him often when he had financial questions."

Financially, the couple took some bold steps as well.

"We decided that we would give with a purpose instead of just simply giving what we felt we could afford," Pia remembers. "However, we weren't really ready to give 10%. So, we decided we would give an extra percent every year."

As the Haglers gave more and more of themselves – their time, talent, and treasure – they began noticing the fruit that it bore in their lives.

"I noticed that the more we gave of ourselves in gratitude, the more we felt blessed," Pia says. "We were getting much closer to our fellow parishioners and the parish, for us, was becoming even more of a tight-knit family than it was before."

Then, one day in 1995, Mike came home and broke the big news to Pia. Msgr. Costigan had decided that, as a parish, St. Mary's would fund all of their ministries through Stewardship, including the parish school. Parishioners' gifts – of time, talent, and treasure – would serve to sustain all parish ministries. The Parish Council had agreed with his decision, and when Mike came home from the meeting he informed Pia that he felt they needed to faithfully give 8% of their gross income to the Church.

"'We can't do that!' I told him," Pia recalls. "It was a very scary thought for me. We had young children and lots of bills. But Mike was determined to make giving to the Church our number one priority, and he convinced me to take a leap of faith together with him."

Pia and Mike have been faithful to their 8% tithe along with their commitments to participate in the life of the parish for many years now, and they have been blown away by the results.

"We've never once looked back, nor have we wanted to look back," Pia says. "Our faith has grown leaps and bounds, and we've been amazed to see that, where financial giving is concerned, making our tithe a first thought and not an afterthought, though sometimes tough, has never left us wanting. It is always there. God always provides, and we feel much more fulfilled."

Pia served for years as the Stewardship Director at St. Mary's, and she watched first-hand as parishioners' lives were changed after embracing Stewardship as a way of life.

"The parish as a whole has changed as a result of Stewardship," Pia says. "It is such a strong family bound by faith and living Christian discipleship together. I feel blessed to call St. Mary's home and to call myself a Christian steward!"

CHAPTER 8

THE LAND OF AHHHS!

St. Martha Catholic Church - Kingwood, Texas

Msgr. Chester Borski
Archdiocese of Galveston-Houston
Pastor of St. Martha Catholic Church Kingwood, TX
Living Stewardship for seven years

Speaking at a Msgr. McGread Stewardship Conference in Wichita, Kansas, Msgr. Chester Borski, the pastor of St. Martha Catholic Church in the Archdiocese of Galveston-Houston, begins his talk on a humorous note.

"There are three things that God does not know," Msgr. Borski states "What a Jesuit is thinking, how much money the Franciscans have, and nowadays He doesn't know how many Stewardship companies there are in the United States. I say that because that is part of the background of how I came to Stewardship. All the pastors here know that every week there is a new company sending you a letter. I just got this one dated February 25th of this year," he says, as he holds a letter in the air. "They are appealing to me as pastor. It says, 'if an increased offertory or Stewardship program is conducted by this company, it promises to be a positive experience for your parish. Our philosophy is to promote the joy of giving that parishioners experience when they are able to help their church. Although no pastor likes asking for money it is often necessary so that ministries can be adequately funded.' Then it goes on to speak about their concept of Stewardship, which is primarily fundraising. But that is not true Stewardship."

Shortly after arriving at St. Martha parish in Kingwood, Texas, Msgr. Borski asked his staff, "when do you have staff meetings?" They looked at him with a blank stare as they responded, "we don't have staff meetings." That answer gave Msgr. Borski his first real glimpse at the kind of parish he was going to be shepherding. St. Martha was a very gifted parish, but it lacked a clear direction. One of the problems Msgr. Borski faced was what he felt was a real lack of adult education available in the parish. "I felt and sensed that most of our people were getting their needs met, in terms of a Scripture study and so forth, but not from the Catholic Church. In fact, many of them were going to the Methodist church and Presbyterian church for some of the Scripture study groups."

Msgr. Borski had been out of parish work for 24 years, serving as the rector for St. Mary's Seminary in

Houston, Texas for 19 of those years. So he knew that he needed time to figure out how God wanted him to serve his new parish. Msgr. Borski spent a couple of months at St. Martha simply observing the needs of the parish before going on a three-and-a-half-month long sabbatical in September 2001. During his sabbatical, he prayed and researched about how he wanted to minister to the St. Martha parish family.

"I was looking for what I called an organizing principle for my ministry and for the ministry at the parish," recalls Msgr. Borski. He was aware that there were many good parish programs available at that time, such as RENEW, a two-year parish-wide program focused on the conversion of hearts. But I wasn't quite sure I wanted to go in a direction of having one program for two years and stopping and retooling and going in another direction," he says. "I figured that at my age I had about another ten to twelve years of ministry if the Lord doesn't take me. And I just didn't feel like I wanted to jump around from one program to another. I wanted to go with some organizing principle that made sense to me personally and would make sense to the people."

So Msgr. Borski began to read and to talk with seasoned pastors throughout the country. He questioned them about the things they were doing in their parishes. He asked them what was working well for them. He attended a parish management seminar as well as a few other workshops, and he read *Excellent Catholic Parishes*, by Paul Wilkes, a book that includes a chapter about St. Francis of Assisi in Wichita as well as other successful parishes.

"I recommend it highly," Msgr. Borski says. "It is an easy read, but gives you a lot of practical ideas." Slowly his thoughts began to clarify and he began to formulate a spiritual plan to bring back to St. Martha. "While I was on sabbatical I came up with three fundamental convictions that would be part of me as I began parish ministry again," he recalls.

Those three convictions were:

1. **We Are Children of God** – "I'm convinced that the most radical thing that can happen to any of us is to be claimed by the Living God to be a child of God. And we are talking about Baptism. I had to really come to that understanding. It really wasn't part of my own formation or education in the early days." But by reading the documents of Vatican II and simply reflecting on life, Msgr. Borski came to understand how Baptism is at the heart of all of our spirituality. "So that is one very basic conviction that I share all the time with our people and I try to live out of that myself."

2. **Renewal Brought About By The Restored Catechumenate** – "The second conviction that I had was that the second most influential document of Vatican II was *Sacrosanctum Concilium*, particularly the section of it that addresses the restored cat-

echumenate or RCIA. If we pay attention to the
process of the catechumenate, we will see that we
are gradually being reshaped as a Church. It is not
just those coming into the Church who are being
renewed, it is all of us as a community being renewed and being challenged by the Gospel about
conversion." While Msgr. Borski said he realized
that the four constitutions – *Gaudium et Spes*, *Lu-
men Gentium*, *Dei Verbum*, and *Sancrosanctum
Concilium* – are all very significant Vatican II documents, he believes that the most practical document from Vatican II for parish life is the one on
the implementation of the catechumenate process.

3. **Importance of Presiding Well During Mass** –
"The third conviction that I came up with while
on sabbatical is that the best way that I can serve
my people is to preside well whenever we cele-
brate Eucharist, especially Sunday Eucharist, and
to preach well. I am not the greatest of preachers.
However, I believe that is the time when I am
most present as pastor to my people. I think we
as pastors, and other priests as well, have a role
of bringing the folks together and this symbolic
role is something I don't think we fully appreci-
ate. The time that I am most present to my people, in the sense of being pastor, I believe, is when
I preside at Eucharist and when I reflect upon the
Scriptures with them."

When he returned to St. Martha in Advent of 2001, Msgr. Borski made it a priority to spend his first year as pastor observing, listening, reading and going through all the information that he had received from different companies about Stewardship. "At the same time, this wasn't the easiest time to be a pastor," he says. The aftermath of September 11 impacted our area. We had also the collapse of Enron. Many of my parishioners were Enron employees as well as some of the other energy companies and finance companies. And compounding these tragic events was the clergy abuse scandal, which was constantly in the news." Msgr. Borski found himself, like many pastors at the time, trying to make sense out of all these challenges, while at the same time still serving as a pastor and a leader of the people.

He had begun to look at Stewardship as his organizing principle for his ministry at St. Martha. "I remember early in the summer of 2003, I received a brochure about the Msgr. McGread Conference that was being held in August of that year. I wasn't quite sure I was going to attend. I had read about Msgr. McGread in several articles and realized he had a vision and a way of presenting Stewardship that was important to consider. Yet I still wasn't sure I would go."

Then, he received a letter from the bishop about an upcoming offertory increase program in the diocese, and Msgr. Borski knew he needed to step into action and look deeper into the Stewardship way of life.

"We got a letter from our bishop saying we were going to go with one of the companies that was appealing to us to increase the offertory collection," Msgr. Borski remembers. "I read their material and it was very positive, but I sensed it was nothing more than primarily a way of increasing the offertory collection."

After talking to a number of pastors, Msgr. Borski felt that if he went in the direction of an offertory increase program he would have to do something else in future years.

"I wondered, 'How do you maintain your parish in terms of the Stewardship model?' And I just didn't want to go there first by asking for money," he says. "I felt that what we needed as a parish community, myself included, was a whole educational approach. And I decided I would focus upon that."

So Msgr. Borski attended the Msgr. McGread Stewardship Conference in August 2003. But even after that, he wasn't totally convinced. He wasn't sure how much of the Stewardship process he could actually implement at St. Martha. However, shortly after he returned from the conference he received a call from the diocesan development director asking for a decision about whether or not he was going to go with one of the offertory increase programs being promoted by the diocese. "So I called part of our Finance Council together as well as a few members from the Pastoral Council," Msgr. Borski says. "We set up a committee. I said we will interview the representative from that company, and then I will make the presentation about what I learned at the Msgr. McGread Stewardship Conference. And that is how we started. I made a presentation, and I showed them the wonderful video of Msgr. McGread's talk. I gave them the handouts that we had received at the conference. And then we listened to the other company. I told the committee, 'You make the decision. You know where I stand. I want to go with an educational approach and not a quick fix. Whether it takes us two, three, five years, whatever it is that is the way I would rather go.' They voted immediately to go with Catholic Stewardship Consultants and the Msgr. McGread approach."

That parish leadership vote was in September. "We then had a meeting with some of our leaders and Eric McArdle from Catholic Stewardship Consultants, and things began to happen much more quickly than I was prepared for. We said let's go with it."

In October of 2003, St. Martha published their first monthly newsletter and mailed it out to all parishioners. "I found that to be a tremendous tool of communication," Msgr. Borski explains. "When I go to the grocery stores and do a little shopping I'm stopped at least five or six times by parishioners. Frequently they will tell me, 'Father I saw this article of what's happening.' And they tell me what is going on. I never got that kind of feedback before from the bulletin. Parishioners read the newsletter, and they let me know what they like and what they don't like about things."

In November 2003, the parish held their first Steward-ship Renewal. The timing was not ideal. Thanksgiving was coming up, the holidays were right around the corner, but the Stewardship Committee felt like they needed to do it. What's more, the Catholic Campaign for Human Develop-ment was held right before Thanksgiving, asking for an increase in the offertory for this national project.

"As pastor, I would have preferred to wait another six months or so," Msgr. Borski admits. "But we went ahead with the Stewardship Renewal with the advice of our committee. The results that came in were a testament to success. We had about 700 Commitment Cards, 3,000 prayer commitments that first time, and 450 ministry commitments. We had done a ministry fair about three months earlier, and many people had already joined new ministries, so that is why the ministry commitments were low because we had already done them before and we only picked out seven ministries that we needed assistance with. There were also about 600 treasure commitments. I did not think that was that great, but Eric assured me that was very good for a parish's first Stew-ardship Renewal. As we proceeded through our first year as a Stewardship parish, I was not concerned about how the offertory was going. In fact, it is very seldom that I look in the bulletin to see how much money we had coming in from the offertory. I should I guess, but it is not that big in my mind. What I am convinced of is the importance of the long-term educational process. Even with the soft sell on the treasure part we had about a 20 to 21% increase in offertory collections."

Other Dimensions of Stewardship at St. Martha:

After the Stewardship Renewal, in February of the following year, St. Martha conducted a Parish Survey. The survey asked parishioners to weigh in about the many parish ministries. They were asked what they wanted and what they needed. Overwhelmingly, they wanted good liturgies, they wanted good adult education, and they identified a need to assist people in need within the immediate community. They already had a soup kitchen, but they wanted the parish to reach out even more. The survey was completed in March 2004, and the results were published in the May newsletter. Then, during Lent 2005,the parish hosted a Leadership Retreat conducted by Catholic Stewardship Consultants. "The retreat was a very positive experience for everyone," Msgr. Borski remembers. "People made comments like, 'I have belonged to the parish for twenty years, and I have never sat at a table before with fellow parishioners and shared faith together;' 'I had seen her as a lector before, but I had never sat at a table with her and shared our dreams and our visions.' It was a great, positive experience. At the same time, in about February or March, we established our Stewardship Committee."

For the first six months of meetings, the Stewardship Committee studied and discussed the bishop's Pastoral

Letter, *Stewardship: A Disciple's Response*. "We would take a chapter a meeting simply to reflect, share experiences, and pray together," Msgr. Borski remembers. "That is all we did. We conducted very little business. Even now, the Stewardship Committee serves as kind of a support system for all of us who are guiding the parish in Stewardship."

During those early meetings, Msgr. Borski took the time to share some of his own Stewardship-related experiences in hopes of impacting the committee members.

"I told them about when I first came to St. Martha," Msgr. Borski explains. "I asked the woman who was in charge of signing people up for envelopes if she could have some sent to me. She said, 'Father you don't have to tithe, you're the pastor.' But I assured her that I wanted to tithe, that, in fact, I needed to tithe, and that I wanted to use the envelopes. Though that was something she had never heard of, she put me down for a set of envelopes, and I used them to contribute on a regular basis. I still do."

As Msgr. Borski recounted the past events with his Stewardship Committee, he discussed with them the importance of doing what he is asking of his parishioners. "I think that is still very critical for all pastors," Msgr. Borski says. "We ask our people to be good stewards, and we need to step up and take that leap of faith ourselves."

Today, the Stewardship Committee meets once a month, and it has grown from eight to ten people.

"We have one couple, both of them are converts," Msgr. Borski explains. "The husband is the son of a Protestant Evangelist, and it was no problem convincing them about tithing. In fact, they have helped us tremendously in our approach to Stewardship. Another one of the committee members took it upon himself to establish a committee called our Planned Giving Committee, because we have a significant number of senior citizens, and we want to make that a long term process as well. And we have also added a member of our Parish Council to be a member, to sit in on the Stewardship Committee."

St. Martha completed their first year of living Stewardship as a way of life in October 2005. It was then time, again, for the Stewardship Renewal.

"The brilliant pastor that I am," Msgr. Borski chuckles, "I decided that we would hold our ministry fair during two weekends rather than one, because last time we didn't have enough room in our Family Life Center. So the first weekend in October we had the Ministry Fair for our outreach ministries, and the second weekend we did our internal ministries – lectors and communion ministers and so forth. I am not going to do that again. Some people chose to go to one and not the other, and I didn't think that was a good experience. Now we do it all at once, but we've expanded it. We use more buildings and so forth and try to create that sense of ministry fair that we want."

During the third weekend Msgr. Borski asked everyone to turn in their Commitment Cards. That year, more than 900 cards were turned in, 4,000 prayer commitments were made, 3,500 ministry commitments and 750 commitments of treasure. What's more, even some of the people who chose not to complete and turn in their Commitment Cards increased their involvement as well.

"Indeed, we still have some education to do in terms of making that written commitment," Msgr. Borski acknowledges. "However, the second year we experienced another 23% increase in terms of participation in the parish. We have experienced an increase in adult education programs. We've even hired a full-time adult education staff member. We have no more space for Little Rock's Scripture series as well as other groups that meet at the parish. There has been an explosion of adults looking to deepen their own faith.

"We've also hired a full-time Spanish-speaking Deacon who heads up our social outreach program and we've joined interfaith prayer partners in the area with the other churches. We also joined another cooperative venture of helping the poor in the community, developed a St. Vincent de Paul Society which had not been present before and have just experienced a lot of enthusiasm from the people to help their fellow citizens, most of whom are not Catholic. It is great to see the participation of the people.

"Our Pastoral Council is developing a strategic pastoral plan, and I have hired architects to develop a master building plan. We don't have enough space for what is going on in the parish and we have to work together with the diocese to see what we can do."

Msgr. Borski assures us that while he is committed to Stewardship, the success at St. Martha is not due to his work, but to the commitment and enthusiasm of the people, and he says that has been a great witness to him.

"The people were waiting to get involved and wanted to get involved. They are very proud to be members of St. Martha parish. They are proud in the community, they are proud with their neighbors that they belong to St. Martha and they are stepping forward to get involved.

"What am I going to do from here? We are going to stay with this Stewardship model. We are going to continue to develop it, emphasizing the fact that all of us are called to live out our Baptismal commitment. One of the things I am committed to is to build strong parish leaders. I had a theologian come speak to our ministers - the catechists, lectors and liturgical ministers. I am going to do that every year. We are also looking at several other projects, evangelization, kind of a parish retreat model called ACTS, but some of these we simply have to hold off on, because we don't have the space to do that."

Though St. Martha's formal Stewardship journey started back in 2003, Msgr. Borski truly believes that it wasn't something new. Rather, living Stewardship is all about going back to the foundation of the Church and the Scriptures and living the Faith. The Stewardship way of life is simply a way of organizing your efforts in this regard.

"I spend a lot of time just focusing upon following in the footsteps of Jesus," Msgr. Borski says. "That is, after all, what our lives as Christian disciples are all about."

PART III

A FINAL NOTE
FOR PARISH LEADERS

CHAPTER 9

JUMP ON THE FLYING CARPET

Are you ready to follow Jesus? Are you ready to live as His disciple today and to bring your fellow parishioners along with you on what is sure to be an amazing journey? No doubt, it will be full of challenges. Your fellow parishioners won't all be enthusiastic from the get go, and some of them may even dramatically resist. But if you listen to Jesus' call and you follow Him, when the times are easy and when they are unbearably tough, then your life and the life of your parish will never be the same!

Are you scared? Are you worried about how your parishioners will react? Are you concerned about your ability to effectively serve as a parish leader in such a life-changing process? Remember, Jesus is the leader. We're all following Him. We just need to trust and do all that we can. He'll take care of the rest.

Do you trust Him?

Imagine that Jesus is standing in front of you. On His right side is a beautiful granite chair and on His left side is a flying carpet. The granite chair looks strong and secure, while the carpet is waving in the breeze.

Jesus looks you in the eyes and calls you by name. "Come to me," He says. You begin to move toward Jesus. He then says, "Come, have a seat."

You visually calculate your options. You could sit on that granite chair – it looks safe and secure, after all – or you could sit on that flying carpet. The carpet may be fun. It may be the start of an amazing adventure, but it sure doesn't look very safe. So you begin moving toward the granite chair. But then Jesus stops you and asks, "Do you trust me?"

"Of course I trust you, Jesus," you reply.

"Then have a seat here," He says, motioning to the flying carpet.

You take a step back, a little fearful and unsure. "Lord, if I try to climb up onto that carpet, I will fall. There is nothing holding it up as it waves in the wind."

But Jesus says once again, "Do you trust me?"

"Yes Lord," you reply.

"Then take a seat on the carpet," Jesus instructs.

You nervously climb onto the carpet, just waiting for it to fall, but, surprisingly, it doesn't. There you sit, on a carpet suspended in the air. You wouldn't believe it if you weren't experiencing it for yourself. As the minutes begin to tick away, your confidence rises and you start to feel pretty good. You even start getting comfortable and feeling safe. Then, Jesus begins to pull out the threads in the carpet one by one by one.

You nervously jump off. "What are you doing Lord? Can't you see I will fall if you keep pulling the threads out?"

Jesus continues to press the question, "Do you trust me?"

"Yes Lord," you reply.

"Then please get back up on the carpet," He says.

You comply with Jesus' request. As you sit on the carpet, Jesus begins to once again pull out the threads – one by one – until there is nothing left. There you sit in the air. No longer is a flying carpet holding you up, but the power of God – a God whom you trusted even when you were unsure of the end results.

Jesus is trying to lead each of us to this point of total and complete trust in Him. The practice of Stewardship helps us to grow in that kind of simple trusting faith in Christ. He promised us He would never abandon us and that He would be with us day-by-day and hour by hour. This kind of simple trusting faith is the kind of faith that St. Francis of Assisi and his Franciscan brothers exemplified. This is the kind of faith that carries us through tough times. This is the kind of faith that the practice of Stewardship helps us grow in by putting God first in our lives – with our use of time, our talents and our financial resources.

The more we grow in this kind of faith, the more peace we have in our lives. This is the kind of faith that Jesus tells us about in the Gospels when he talked about how our Heavenly Father cares for the birds of the air and the grass in the field and how much more He cares about us.

"For this reason I say to you, do not be worried about your life, as to what you will eat or what you will drink; nor for your body, as to what you will put on. Is not life more than food, and the body more than clothing? "Look at the birds in the sky; they do not sow, nor reap nor gather into barns, and yet your heavenly Father feeds them. Are not you more important than they? "And who of you by being worried can add a single hour to his life? And why are you worried about clothing? Observe how the lilies of the field grow; they do not toil nor do they spin, yet I say to you that not even Solomon R213 in all his glory clothed himself like one of these. But if God so clothes the grass of the field, which is alive today and tomorrow is thrown into the furnace, will He not much more clothe you? You of little faith! Do not worry then, saying, `What will we eat?' or `What will we drink?' or `What will we wear for clothing?' For the Gentiles eagerly seek all these things; for your heavenly Father knows that you need all these things. But seek first His king-

dom and His righteousness, and all these things will be added to you.

(Matthew 6:25-33)

This is the kind of faith that Msgr. Thomas McGread is convinced comes from living a life of Stewardship. This is the kind of faith that has inspired so many parishes around the country to follow in Msgr. McGread's footsteps.

Will you follow? Will you accept the challenge? Trust Jesus. Jump on the flying carpet! The rewards are everlasting.

PRACTICAL TOOLS AND PROCESSES

Below you will find a list of the key elements that we at Catholic Stewardship Consultants believe are necessary for any parish or diocese who wants to successfully implement the Stewardship way of life. I have also included some recommendations that I believe will make the usage of the tools and processes I have listed affective for your parish and/or diocese. (The information in this appendix is reprinted from Catholic Stewardship Consultants' Msgr. McGread Conference booklet.)

Communicating the Stewardship Message

It is extremely important that there be an integration of the parish's stewardship message through all of its communication outlets, which include the parish's printed materials. As your parish travels through its stewardship journey, you must be careful that you do not have a disjointed effort. Some parishes, often early in their stewardship journey or when they have reached a plateau, begin to start "shooting from the hip" in regards to their stewardship efforts. At times, parishes begin to try one thing after another, but instead of hitting on one solution, these parishes often confuse their parishioners. Each parish needs to have a primary goal in mind and then be able to work on each step toward that goal, while realizing their goal will take time.

Annual Planning

Parishes need to create an annual plan that establishes concrete goals, schedules and responsibilities for the entire year. Such a plan will help to guide the entire stewardship initiative by detailing each component of the process, when it will be conducted, and who is responsible.

In addition to the annual plan, those responsible for implementing stewardship should collaborate with the parish leaders to prayerfully envision the next several years of parish stewardship development to ensure steady growth in the stewardship way of life.

Parish Newsletters

Most parishes rely on their weekly bulletin to communicate information about parish activities. Although these weekly bulletins serve their purpose, they do have their limitations. The information communicated in the weekly bulletin is only communicated with those who attend Mass on a given Sunday, which is not the entire parish family. Also, the bulletin can only communicate a very limited amount of information. It may have a short paragraph regarding when the Knights of Columbus are meeting or some other parish event, but it doesn't give people a real sense of the life of the parish. The information in the bulletin often helps remind those already involved in the parish about parish activities, but it doesn't draw in those parishioners who are not yet involved.

Parish newsletters help to enhance the parish's communication with its parishioners – all of its parishioners. Newsletters are able to share more detailed information about parish groups, parish people, parish traditions, parish plans, etc. Instead of a short paragraph about when the Knights of Columbus are meeting next, the newsletter might explain who the Knights of Columbus are and what they do within the parish and the community. Most parishioners receive newsletters very warmly. However, most parishes find that newsletters can be hard to maintain without committed help either from very committed and talented parishioners or a professional firm. In fact, it is better to not even start a newsletter than to start one and then stop it a few months later or to start one that is prepared inconsistently or amateurishly.

Parish newsletters should be:

- **Consistent** – They should be mailed out on a consistent basis. Parishioners should know when to expect them.

- **Mailed to Homes** – This enables all parish members to receive a parish newsletter, not just those who come to Mass on Sunday. It lets all of your parishioners know that they are a part of the parish and may encourage fallen away Catholics to begin to go back to Mass

- **Of High Quality** – The written content and the design, as well as the paper that the newsletter is printed on, should be of high quality. Amateurish newsletters give the feeling of an amateurish parish. A high quality, professional looking, and well written newsletter gives those who receive it a good impression of the parish. A high quality newsletter also encourages parishioners who receive it to actually read it.

- **Include Photos** – Photos of different parishioners and parish activities help to visually connect parishioners with the parish. Pictures also add interest to the visual appeal of the newsletter.

- **Regular Content** – The newsletter should contain different sub-sections, columns that remain consistent over time.

Parish Surveys

Many parishioners do not feel that their opinions/thoughts matter. In reality, without the parishioners there would be no parish. There are different times in the life of a parish when a parish survey, if effectively developed and implemented, is needed. Maybe your parish is considering building a new church, but you don't know how many parishioners would be supportive. Or maybe you want to know what types of parish groups are needed within the parish. Also, pastors often hear from the parishioners who yell the loudest. Maybe you are hearing a lot of negative feedback, and you think that the whole parish feels the same way. Then a parish survey can be helpful.

You might find that the loud and negative portion of your parishioners only makes up 2% of the parish, or that the parish will not support the building of a new church right now, or that more adult education is desperately needed. A parish survey is a vehicle through which you can listen to some of the general needs, concerns and thoughts within the parish. Unfortunately, many parish surveys conduct dust. If parishioners participate in a survey, but don't feel that they are heard or that no action was taken, then they will become more disconnected from the parish in the future.

In order to be effective, a parish survey should:

- Be thoughtfully developed based on your particular parish's needs and concerns.
- Have a professional look and grammatically correct content.
- Be mailed to all parishioners' homes. Remember that in-pew surveys only reach the people who

come to Mass on a particular Sunday – not the entire parish.

- Include a return envelope.
- Have results that are compiled and then communicated to all of the parishioners. Parishioners
  need to know that they were heard and what the
  results were. Are other parishioners concerned
  about similar things?
- Include analysis of the results before taking action. Let the parishioners know that their voices
  were not only heard, but the parish is taking particular actions due to their responses. This helps
  the parishioners to feel a stronger sense of ownership in what the parish decides to do.
- Remind parishioners to return their parish surveys because their participation is important.
  This reminder could be done through the parish
  newsletter, announcements at Mass, the bulletin,
  etc.

Spiritual Leadership Retreats

Strong lay leaders are vital for every parish. They
provide the pastor with valuable insight and they also
serve as examples for the rest of the parish. For these
reasons, it is critical that lay leaders understand stewardship and practice it in their lives, because stewardship is
essentially a faith response.

Because practicing stewardship is essentially a faith response, we have found that a retreat setting which incorporates talks, prayer, reflection and group discussions works exceptionally well in cultivating strong parish leadership. It provides a time for all the parish leaders to draw aside and spend time with God and with one another. It is an opportunity for them to reflect on the parish's future direction and their roles as parish leader. However, the purpose of the retreat is to foster personal conversion in a stewardship context, not to provide a leadership training workshop or a strategic planning session.

Stewardship Committee Development

An active Stewardship Committee is crucial, because strong leadership is a hallmark of a stewardship parish.

An effective Stewardship Committee works to understand the foundations of stewardship and to extend that understanding and its practice throughout the parish. Members should be carefully chosen based on their current commitment and willingness to grow.

The Stewardship Committee can be an invaluable asset in many aspects of parish life, including the Annual Stewardship Renewal, organizing a Ministry Fair, and promoting stewardship in other parish organizations and ministries.

Annual Stewardship Renewals

Renewals are an important part of our lives – whether they take place in our marriage, in our profession, or in our spirituality. The need for renewal extends to the promotion of stewardship. Planning and implementing an Annual Stewardship Renewal can, however, seem overwhelming. But it is a very important step in making stewardship a way of life within your parish. The Annual Stewardship Renewal offers your parishioners an opportunity to grow in their ongoing faith journey. It involves inviting your parishioners to make a commitment to the parish – return a portion of their Time, Talent, and Treasure back to God.

> "People who plan their religious giving on an annual basis, rather than by looking at their checkbook each Sunday to see what they can afford that week, contribute more." (Why Catholics Don't Give...And What Can Be Done About It, 2nd edn., Dr. Charles E. Zech, pg. 132).

The Annual Stewardship Renewal is a chance to remind parishioners of their responsibilities as disciples of Christ, to explain the parish's practice of stewardship over the last year, to highlight the parish's plans for the next year, and then invite them to commit to being involved. Many parishes have different approaches to this Annual Renewal, but we have found the following to be extremely important.

- **Plan** – Enough can't be said about planning for the Annual Renewal. Your parish's plans will ultimately determine the success of your Renewal. Planning involves what will be done, when it will be done, and who will do it. When will the Renewal be held? What will it involve? How will returned results be compiled? How will the results be followed up on? Your Annual Renewal could comprise a 3-week period where:
    - 1st Week – Pastor speaks about stewardship, focusing on Time and Talent. Conduct a Time and Talent Fair.
    - 2nd Week – Lay witnesses talk. This sharing of a parishioner's or parishioners' personal faith story and their experience with stewardship, including their struggles, encourages other parishioners. Stewardship Renewal packets are mailed to all homes.
    - 3rd Week – Pastor concludes, and Commitment Cards should be returned.
- **Printed Materials** – It is important that all printed materials be attractive, professional looking, and visually coordinated. After all, you are communicating information about God's invitation to all of your parishioners. This information will also be competing with many other messages for your parishioners' attention. These materials should include:

- Cover letter signed by the pastor in the renewal packet.
- Brochure that outlines the general concept of stewardship and the parish's particular stewardship message.
- Listing of Parish Ministries/Groups
- Commitment Card and Envelope which allows parishioners to respond to the invitation by writing down their Time, Talent, and Treasure commitments.

- **Reminder to Participate** – This can be done in the bulletin, through announcements at Mass, in the newsletter, and by mailing out reminder cards.
- **Follow Up with Those Who Have Not Returned Their Commitment Cards** – This may involve phones calls to see if the stewardship packet was received, follow-up mailings, home visitations, etc.
- **Follow Up with Those Who Have Returned Their Commitment Cards**– This may involve:
  - Sending thank you cards to everyone who returned their Commitment Card.
  - Recording the commitments into a computerized program.
  - Giving a list of those who committed to parish ministries to the particular parish leaders.

- Having a plan for the parish leaders to follow-up with each individual through a personal telephone call that invites them to the next group event.
- **Communicate Results to the Parish** – This may be done in the newsletter, etc.
- **Analyzing the Results** – This includes comparing this year's results with last year's results on a parish-wide basis as well as by each family.

Measuring the Results

In order to effectively measure the results of the Annual Stewardship Renewal, it is critical for the parish to have good records. You might want to compare the following:

- Total Treasure Committed – The difference between this year and last year.
- Total Treasure by Families – The difference between this year and last year with a listing of each parish family and their individual gifts.
- Number of Commitment Cards Received
- Number of Commitments for each Parish Group/Ministry
- Listing of New Commitments